Conflict Resolution

Its Language and Processes

John W. Burton

D0792743

The Scarecrow Press, Inc.
Lanham, Md., & London
1996

SCARECROW PRESS, INC.

Published in the United States of America
by Scarecrow Press, Inc.
4720 Boston Way
Lanham, Maryland 20706

4 Pleydell Gardens, Folkestone
Kent CT20 2DN, England

British Cataloguing-in-Publication Information Available

Library of Congress Cataloging-in-Publication Data

Burton, John W. (John Wear), 1915–
    Conflict resolution : its language and processes / John W. Burton.
        p.   cm.
    Includes bibliographical references and index.
    ISBN 0–8108–3265–8 (cloth : alk. paper) ISBN 0–8108–3214–3 (pbk :
    alk. paper)
        1. Conflict management. 2. Conflict manangement—Terminology.
I. Title.
HM136.B786   1996
303.6'9—dc20   96–9224
                                                                  CIP

ISBN 0–8108–3265–8 (cloth : alk.paper)
ISBN 0–8108–3214–3 (pbk : alk.paper)

⊖™ The paper used in this publication meets the minimum requirements of
American National Standard for Information Sciences—Permanence of
Paper for Printed Library Materials, ANSI Z39.48–1984.

*To parents, teachers, managers, lawyers,
diplomats, and politicians.*

Contents

Preface

We are all today greatly concerned with increasing levels of conflict and violence, in our own localities and around the globe. Containing violence by national and international policing has not succeeded. Getting to the source of conflict and violence at all social levels and avoiding the conditions that provoke social problems is challenging, but at stake are quality of life in the present, and, ultimately, the future of civilizations. It is a challenge that must be accepted.

A shift from authoritative containment to problem solving and problem avoidance is made possible by discoevering where we have gone wrong, and evolving a more reliable theory of behaviors from which to deduce the means of resolving and avoiding problems. This leads to a new set of assumptions and, therefore, to a new language and radically different processes.

There have now been thirty years of appropriate theory development and exploratory practice, and there are many student texts. But conflict and violence are of general concern, not just that of a few specialists. On the contrary, until specialists manage to communicate their thinking, and unless this alternative approach becomes a consensus, their goals will not be achieved. This book seeks to provide an understanding of the concepts, language, and processes of a problem-solving approach.

I wish to acknowledge the positive contributions made by the 1995 and 1996 graduate students of the Centre for Conflict Resolution at the Macquarie University, Sydney, and their mentors Andrew Heys, Dr. Alan Tidwell, and Dr. Greg Tillett.

1
Problem-Solving Conflict Resolution

Introduction

Conflict and violence within societies, and conflicts between them over territories and resources, are a part of history. Tradition and conventional wisdom have held that such dissident and antisocial behaviors are to be controlled and prevented by education, backed by punitive action. At the international level, aggressive behaviors are to be contained by power balances and by international institutions.

At no stage have such controls been highly effective. And now, both at national and international levels, violence, made even more effective by new technologies, is out of control.

Empirical evidence suggests that a great deal of conflict and violence is provoked by such circumstances as childhood environments, the absence of job opportunities, insecurities experienced because of a minority status, resource deprivations, and postcolonial boundaries that cut through ethnic communities. To the extent that this is so the remedy must be to deal with these problems at their source by whatever structural changes are required, thereby resolving specific problems and preventing others from occurring.

Such problem-solving and problem-avoidance policies would have to take into account all behavioral, cultural, institutional, and environmental circumstances. This would seem to be beyond human capacities, too idealistic to contemplate. In the last hundred years, specializations in social sciences have evolved to avoid just these complexities and to become more quantitative and "scientific."

But specializations have failed us. A remedy for a specific problem may have sideeffects causing others. For example, economic and financial policies designed to control inflation and to promote investment have adverse consequences, such as youth unemployment and associated crime. More and more social sciences are finding that they must cross boundaries and be more holistic in approach.

Holism is not idealism. It is realism, the kind of comprehensive diagnostic realism we would all welcome when visiting our family doctor. Societies are a total of interactive social relationships. Resolving and avoiding problems must take into account behaviors at all social levels, from the family to the international. They must embrace the totality of knowledge about human relationships and the total environment in which these relationships exist. Such holism is not difficult for us to understand: it reflects our personal observations and intuitive assessments.

The Problem Area

All societies are characterized by social conventions that seek to make possible continuing orderly patterns of behavior. Social norms have evolved in different circumstances, leading to different cultures.

Historically, the more privileged and influential members of societies have played a major role in determining norms, and in having them observed by others. With the evolution of democracies there have been continuous trends toward more broadly agreed upon norms. Their observance, while promoted by education, is, nevertheless, still backed by deterrent strategies and punishments as was the case with more elite-dominated societies.

The evolutionary shift toward more widely agreed norms and processes has brought with it a weakening of enforcement possibilities, for they also are subject to wider scrutiny. Doubt is now cast on the value of punishment as a deterrent. Furthermore, technological developments have provided means of resistance, making possible individual defiance of social norms and of authorities whose role it is to enforce them.

The present is, therefore, a crucial transition stage in human evolution. The traditional coercive basis of law and order on which societies have rested is no longer effective.

As yet societies have tended to push the problem aside, relying on more police and jails, more forces and weapons of mass destruction. But the availability of these same means of repression to those who are being controlled leads to increased capabilities of defiance of authorities.

There are many reasons why this problem has not been tackled. The first is, understandably, the view that anti-social behaviors should be controlled by methods which seem to have "worked" in the past that merely need to be updated and made more efficient. Rather than move toward untried alternatives it is deemed preferable to maintain the status quo, regardless of immediate costs.

The second is the nature of the challenge. Any rejection of social norms, and resistance to authorities whose duty it is to enforce them, have traditionally been held to be immoral and unethical, being a failure to observe those values supported by religions and cultural belief systems. Any suggestion that there may be valid reasons for divergences, any suggestion that existing institutions and structures may themselves be a source of crime and violence requiring, therefore, fundamental changes, is too challenging to those who value traditional institutions. Such people include many who are underprivileged as well as power elites. Rather than change, they prefer the option of increased security measures provided by authorities and, when they can afford it, by themselves.

Closely associated with this resistance to change on the basis of tradition there is a powerful intellectual resistance. In his review of utopias, Lewis Mumford[1] observes that "In negative form, the utopian ideal of total control from above, absolute obedience below, never entirely passed out of existence."

A False Assumption

There is a hidden assumption here, that the human person is wholly malleable and is capable of conforming with institutional requirements. All social science disciplines have tended to accept this assumption. Economists treat the person as a machine: unemployed youth can and should accept the absence of the identity a job could give. Sociologists have been concerned with means by which the person can be persuaded to adapt to social institutions. Even psychologists have been more concerned with helping the person to adapt to society than with pointing to changes required in social norms and institutions.

We will be arguing that this assumption of malleability is probably false. If this is so there is an explanation of why deterrence does not reliably deter, why there is a failure to maintain law and order in communities, and why great powers can be defeated in wars with small nations. There may be a limit to the human capacity to adapt, leading to resistance to the point of self-sacrifice. This raises the question, what are the alternatives?

Conflict Analysis

As a consequence of such questioning there evolved during the late 1970s a significant literature on "Conflict Analysis and Resolution."[2] This was not utopian idealism. It was, rather, essentially a costing analysis. Resolution was seen as possible, not through goodwill and an altered value system, but by a realistic analysis of situations and an assessment of the costs and consequences of policies that were based on false assumptions and perceptions.

Conflict analysis first sought the explanation for the failure of traditional power-elite, deterrent strategies. To do so there had to be examinations of conflicts at all social levels—family, ethnic, industrial and international. The research processes included bringing together parties to conflicts, helping them to be analytical, and observing their responses.[3]

The conflicting parties concerned in this research seemed to benefit from the exercise. Accordingly, the research process was modified to become a conflict resolving process. A decade or so later sources of conflict were becoming clearer. Teaching centers and institutes for "Conflict Analysis and Resolution" were established.[4]

Perhaps the most significant discovery made during this period was that the goals that could not be compromised were shared common human aspirations. There were "human needs" of identity and recognition that kept surfacing, leading to behaviors that could be violent as, for example, the pursuit of secession by minorities, and of independence by colonial peoples. Being inherent these needs were shared needs. Once they were mutually recognized by the parties concerned in a particular conflict, and once it was realized that no relative power position could eliminate the problem, viable options were eagerly explored. Details of the processes seemed to be required by theory and experience were published.[5]

This book seeks, first, to explain the language used in presenting these alternatives, and in so doing to help to explain the alternatives themselves, and second, to outline in practical detail problem-solving means of dealing with specific conflicts and social problems.

Notes

1. *Utopias and Utopian Thought* edited by Frank E. Manuel (New York: Souvenir Press, 1965) p. 19.

2. For example, see Select Bibliography.

3. Parties in conflict were brought together in Southeast Asia, Cyprus, Lebanon, Falklands and elsewhere. See an article by Ronald Fisher in *Beyond Confrontation,* edited by John A. Vasquez and colleagues (Ann Arbor, Mi.: University of Michigan Press, 1995).

4. There are centers and institutes for conflict resolution in many countries, including Australia, Canada, India, South Africa, the United Kingdom, the United States, and many others, and courses taught in many more.

5. See John W. Burton, *Resolving Deep-Rooted Conflict: A Handbook* (Lanham, Md., University Press of America, 1987). Also an appendix in *Conflict: Practices in Management, Settlement and Resolution,* John Burton and Frank Dukes (New York:St.Martin's; London: Macmillan, London, 1990).

2

The Language of Conflict Resolution

In all social relationships there are inevitably ongoing differences in viewpoints. These emerge in *discussions* and opinions may change. Discussions may lead to *arguments*. Their settlement is usually by dialogue, frequently assisted by persons with an open mind, leading to altered opinions. Indeed, research dialogue is characterized by arguments, leading to discovery and to increased knowledge.

In many social relationships there are also *disputes* over contending interests, especially material interests. These, also, may be settled by discussion, but are more likely to require mediation by a neutral party. In recent years great improvements have been made in the settlement of disputes. Processes now include adjudication, arbitration, mediation, negotiation, and combinations of these. Whenever compromise is willingly acceptable, disputes can be settled without further deterioration in relationships.

Conflicts are struggles between opposing forces, implying that the issues are more serious than those relating to disputes, possibly stimulating physical confrontations.

Although dictionaries make such a distinction between "disputes" and "conflicts," in practice they are treated as one. The reason is that consensual conceptions do not include any clear understanding of why and in what respects disputes and conflicts differ in intensity.

With no conceptual distinction made between the nature of disputes and conflicts, the dispute settlement processes have been applied to all situations, whether minor differences or serious confrontations.

The dispute-settlement processes include bargaining and negotiation, and also some degree of persuasion and coercion. Parties may feel that they have no option but to accept outcomes, perhaps because of the stronger bargaining power of the other side, perhaps because of legal norms being applied within the mediation process, perhaps because of the costs of taking the matter further by court action. Despite this element of forced acceptance of outcomes, it is assumed that outcomes will be observed.

In many cases there is "settlement," but problems recur. There are cases in which forced compromise leaves the problem as it was before arbitration or mediation. For example, a custody argument is likely to be settled in favor of the mother. A father can be left with a sense of frustration that finds expression in some desperate action. A wage dispute can be settled by some wage increase, but may not reveal unstated reasons for the claim, such as unacceptable working conditions or denigrating treatment by employers. At other social levels there are problems in relationships arising out of perceived ethnic or gender discrimination, which usually cannot be settled within existing institutional and political structures. The outcome of arbitration and mediation is likely to be one that merely suppresses resentments for the time being.

Experience has thus drawn attention to differences between "disputes," which can be settled by compromise, and "conflicts," which involve issues on which there cannot be compromise. At all social levels, from the family to the international, there are problems in social relationships that involve emotions and deep-seated needs in respect of which there can be no compromise. Such conflicts must be *resolved*, rather than *settled*. The dispute-settlement processes are inappropriate. Analytical processes are required that uncover the sources of the problem and deal with them accordingly.

Conflicts occur both at and across all social levels. A major type of conflict has always been between authorities and those individuals and communities over whom authorities exercise control. Both traditionally and in modern societies a basic proposition has been that there are, at all social levels and in all institutions, those who have acquired the right to control, leaving others with an obligation to obey. Within this power frame the emergence of issues over which there cannot be compromise must lead to violence. Such instances of violence may be termed "terrorism" from one perspective, "the pursuit of human needs" from another.

All modern cultures, that is, those that are no longer small, face-to-face societies, share forms of such authoritative control. In Western cultures there have been landlords and serfs, employers and employees, and indigenous peoples and those who have taken over their territories. Western societies now have an upper or upper-middle class which provides decision makers with resulting theories and policies that play to their interests. Other cultures have their own forms of elite control. In all cases conformity rests finally on threats of punishment and deterrent strategies.

It is within this context that societies continue to operate within systems governed by power and characterized by adversarial institutions: adversarial party politics, adversarial legal processes, adversarial workplace relationships, and adversarial relationships between sovereign authorities and minorities seeking separate autonomies. Collaborative problem-solving processes are frequently resisted by those holding power insofar as they might pose the threat of social and institutional change.

Herein lies the core of the problem civilizations face. The failure to define *disputes* and *conflicts*, and the treatment of conflicts as though all issues in human relationships are negotiable and subject to compromise, lead to attempts at forced "settlement" within existing institutional and social norms. This, along with little concern for the structures and conditions that were the causes of the conflictual behaviors in the first place, is the major source of violence in societies.

This age-old problem of conflict in societies now takes on a new dimension. The weapons of power are now of unlimited capacity and widely available. Power has taken on a new meaning. It is no longer in the hands only of those who have "earned" the right to govern. Even the powerful are threatened by the assumed weaker nations and peoples, all of whom have means of resistance.

Furthermore, the social conditions of conflict are deteriorating at an exponential rate: ethnic minorities making demands for autonomy, population doubling in thirty-five years or less, increased resource scarcities, environmental contamination.

Civilizations thus face an unprecedented challenge. Can there be a turnaround from the kind of societies in which conditions of conflict are promoted, toward systems in which human intellectual capabilities can be employed to promote problem solving rather than problem suppression? Can human intelligence be employed to determine the future of civilizations now that uncontrolled evolution is pointing in the direction of the demise of civilizations?

Resolution by getting to the sources of a problem logically shifts thinking from resolving a specific conflict toward processes by which all such conflicts can be avoided in the future. This brings conflict resolution and conflict prevention into the field of decision making and public policy.

Any shift in thinking requires a new language. This problem-solving approach unavoidably has its own language. Special meanings have been given to *disputes* and *conflicts*. Similar precision must be given to *mediation* which still means different processes to different people. *Resolution* often means, not resolving a problem, but peacekeeping or police action: getting to the sources and "resolving" a conflict is not a part of accepted thinking. Indeed, even some scholars working in this area use these terms interchangeably. Instead of "dispute settlement" and "conflict resolution," "conflict settlement" and "dispute resolution" are widely employed to describe processes.

Advances in understanding have led to more precise definitions of terms, to alterations in meaning, and to new terms. This is part of the normal process of discovery: new concepts make neccesary new meanings and new terms. The alteration of the meaning of words is an ongoing process. For instance, *anarchy* is now defined as lawlessness and disorder, yet the original meaning is reflected in the dictionary definition of an anarchist as a person who advocates a system based on voluntary cooperation, implying an ideal state in which law and its enforcement are not required. The invention of new words is also an ongoing process. For example, the term *provention* has recently been introduced to signify getting to the sources of conflict and taking measures to avoid conflict, including alterations in institutions and social policies, rather than just *preventing* conflict by deterrent threat or suppression.

More important, within the emerging conflict resolution frame there are terms that have an altered connotation. For example, in a power-elite frame, behavior that is "ethical" relates to the observance of the legal, social, or religious norms of a particular society. In a conflict resolution frame, the concept "ethics" means behaviors that do not damage in any way the self-esteem, sense of identity, and role of the individual, but, on the contrary, help to promote them. It is, therefore, a concept that cuts across cultures.

In the past, new terms have reflected extensions to existing practice, for example, from legal processes to "alternative dispute resolution," meaning out-of-court or before-court processes. But with conflict resolution we are not dealing just with extensions of practice. We are dealing with a fundamental paradigm shift in thinking and, therefore, in practice. It is a total shift from the various procedures within a power frame to processes by which there can be a thorough analysis of the sources and nature of a situation, leading to means of determining whether the situation is a dispute or a conflict, to means of resolving it if it is a conflict, and of preventing its occurrence in the future. Such a fundamental shift can come about only by education at all levels, from the small child to the postgraduate, the industrial manager, the civil servant, and the statesman. As a mode of thought it is no less relevant to doctors, lawyers, and all who work with humans and their systems. Although there are relevant courses in many universities, these cater primarily to students with a special interest in the subject. But it is a study that intellectually belongs to any social science concerned with decisionmaking, be it international relations, management studies, politics, sociology, or psychology.

But first there is the need for a new language. Distinctions must be made between general usage and the special meanings implied within the frame of conflict resolution.

A study of language shortens the discovery and learning process. It provides the language of the theories and practices of dispute settlement and conflict resolution as they are emerging, and in this way helps to promote more quickly an understanding of the nature of disputes and conflicts and the processes that are relevant.

Although the purpose of such a "dictionary" of conflict resolution is to focus on terms that have altered meanings in the context of conflict resolution, it also includes many terms which are not within the area of conflict resolution, such as compromise, which relate to dispute settlement. In this way the distinction made between conflicts and disputes, and their relevant processes, is made clearer.

3
Selected Terms

A

Abduction. The term *induction*, meaning a process of reasoning by which a conclusion is drawn from a set of premises based on empirical experience, and the term *deduction*, meaning a process of reasoning by which a conclusion logically follows from a set of premises based on theoretical explanations, are both in general use. When there is a major questioning of consensus ideas and of the widely accepted assumptions on which they rest, neither relying on empirical evidence nor on general premises can provide an adequate process of reasoning. Last century a mathematical philosopher, C. S. Peirce (d. 1914) introduced the term *abduction* to suggest a process by which empirical evidence and theories, frequently reflecting personal prejudices in their selection and interpretations, would be challenged by intuition and insights derived from all available knowledge. In his terms this was "critical commonsensism," which he called *abduction.*

Conflict resolution is a study that cuts across all social levels, and, therefore, all social disciplines. For this reason it challenges widely held concepts and fundamental assumptions, as will be seen from redefinitions in this dictionary. It rests on both empirical evidence and deduced theories, but always within the context of total knowledge rather than that which is limited by disciplinary boundaries. For this reason it is abductive.

Adisciplinary. *Multidisciplinary* is widely used to suggest the coming together of two or more separate studies or disciplines in some particular area. For example, psychology and social science might bring their separate perspectives to focus on a specific problem, such as juvenile street gangs. Conflict resolution seeks to be holistic in two senses. First, it seeks to deal with a particular problem by relating it to the totality of social problems; for example, gangs and crime are related to juvenile unemployment and to family problems, which in turn relate to education, health, etc. Second, in examining these related problem areas, it seeks to include all behavioral elements, psychological, economic, political, sociological, etc. In this latter goal it seeks to cut across all discipline boundaries, and is, therefore, *adisciplinary*.

Adjudication. To *adjudicate* is to give a formal or binding decision, not necessarily by a judge. A referee adjudicates. In this sense it is an alternative to a court decision, but requires a formal status. In some contexts a mediator approximates this role, especially when formally given an "Alternative Dispute Settlement" role. In a conflict resolution role, by contrast, there is no judging role and the term is not employed in this context.

Adversarial. *Adversarial* is a term normally used to apply to persons and members of groups and political parties who are in opposition and who act accordingly. It is not a condition that is universally condemned. On the contrary, being adversarial is frequently admired, as in political leadership. It is not, therefore, a term usually applied critically to the basic institutions of society, such as politics, law, and the workplace where being adversarial is regarded as essential to democracy and to decision making.

In an alternative problem-solving or conflict-re-solving frame it is a derogatory term. The existence of adversarial relationships invites a reconsideration of the confrontational institutions concerned. Politicians, lawyers, and industrial managers may not be adversarial as persons, but are frequently required to be adversarial by the structures in which they operate.

Alienation. *Alienate* usually has the meaning to become hostile, to become unfriendly, to turn away. *Alienation* is the end result of processes or relationships that alienate.

In conflict resolution there is frequently a focus on alienation to describe the feelings of those who are alienated. The source of the condition is not usually an interpersonal relationship, or the experience of personal hostility. It refers to the condition in which individuals experience a sense of exclusion from society, maybe because of unemployment or lack of a social role. Being alienated results in a loss of identity and personal recognition and is directly linked to antisocial behaviors, such as joining a street gang as a means of securing identity and having a role in society.

Alternative Dispute Resolution. *Alternative Dispute Resolution* (ADR) is a phrase that emerged in the 1970s to describe mediated out-of-court or before-court interactions between parties to a dispute or conflict. Some judges in the United States require such processes to be followed before appearance in their courts. ADR typically lacks any analytical process. Frequently it makes no distinction between disputes and conflicts. It tends to apply exisiting legal norms in this more informal way. With more knowledge of conflict resolution this may be changing. The title is misleading: *settlement* would be more appropriate than *resolution*.

Analysis. *Analysis* implies breaking down the whole into its constituent parts so as to examine their features and relationships. *Psycho*analysis seeks to identify particular experiences that might affect behavior.

Conflict resolution employs *analysis* frequently, even to describe the nature of an institution, e.g. "Institute for Conflict Analysis and Resolution," but the meaning intended is to suggest being holistic rather than separating out aspects of behaviors and relationships. Parties in conflict are brought together so that they can reperceive and redefine their relationships in ways that correct limited perspectives and provide a holistic explanation of behaviors. Two parties could be in conflict because each perceives the behavior of the other as being aggressive. A searching analysis will reveal the explanation of the apparent aggressive behaviors. Frequently this will relate to shared deprivations and concerns touching on identity and independence in decision making. Analysis separates conflict resolution from processes of bargaining, negotiation and mediation which rarely reveal the underlying issues that are the source of the conflict.

Anarchy. *Anarchy* is a good example of a term acquiring an altered meaning. Originally it had the meaning of the absence of formal legal processes. Authoritative law in a face-to-face community was unnecessary. The term acquired a negative connotation when enforced law and order became the foundation of larger societies.

Today, secession movements and separate autonomies are frequently interpreted as being anarchy or leading to anarchy within the nation-state system. Within a behavioral frame, separate autonomies may be the means of avoiding conflict and promoting harmonious functional relationships among different identity groups—a condition reflected in the original meaning of anarchy. But the contemporary trend toward smaller political units and more community decision making seems, mistakenly, to attract the description anarchy, meaning chaos.

Assimilation.   One of the most important sources of conflict and violence in the contemporary global system relates to ethnic, racial, tribal, religious, and other identity groupings that are within the same nation-state boundaries. Within a power frame, *assimilation* is designed to provide social harmony among different identity groups.

In the colonial era these problems were contained by the policies of colonial powers. In particular, minorities, which valued the protection of the colonial power, were made responsible for administrative services and the police control of majorities. With independence, majorities took control and discrimination against minorities became widespread, leading to demands for autonomy.

A contradictory global trend has been the influx of migrants and refugees into developed countries. Different languages and cultures, and identification with factions at war with each other within countries of origin, have been accepted as inevitable. Little thought has been given to the question whether the absence of assimilation and the development of multiculturalism within these developed countries will, as populations grow, lead to the same kind of violent conflict.

In these changing circumstances the two terms *assimilation* and *multiculturalism* have become confused, sometimes used interchangeably. This confusion tends to divert attention away from policies that might be designed actively to promote greater assimilation, for example, the avoidance of geographic concentrations of peoples of the same culture that lead to concentrations in schools and in local activities and to a slower rate of learning the local language and social norms.

In a conflict resolution frame, in which identity is treated as an inherent human need, assimilation is an unrealistic conception in the absence of planned educational and social policies to promote it. There are few examples of planned assimilation, leaving multiculturalism still in doubt as a viable option, at least in the absence of conditions that provide identity and remove insecurity. See **Multiculturalism.**

Autonomy.   *Autonomy* implies the right of self-determination and self-government, or freedom to determine one's own actions. In the power frame it has limited use or relevance, particularly at the international level at which defense of sovereignty is still regarded as the first priority. Minorities that seek autonomy are to be repressed in defense of sovereignty.

In changing global circumstances in which communications and means of resistance are readily available, demands for autonomy are widespread. Secession movements are a major symptom of ethnic conflict. This is largely a post-World War II phenomenon and little thought has been given to possible forms of autonomy. They could vary from complete independence and new sovereignties, to limited control of education and related cultural elements.

Conflict resolution processes necessarily explore possibilities in specific cases. Far greater importance is attached to the notion of autonomies than is the case in any power negotiation. The human needs for identity are recognized and brought to the surface in conflict resolution processes. When it is realized that autonomy relates directly to the need for separate identity, evident in the behavior even of children from the age of two or so, the costs and consequences of maintaining sovereignty by coercive means become clearer. Options are explored.

B

Behavior. In a power frame, *behavior* means the manner of behaving, or the actual response of an organism or machine to some stimulus. There are studies of behavior that seek to make objective studies of human behaviors. But such definitions and studies, because of the power frame and assumptions about individual abilities to conform with legal and social norms, pay little attention to inherent drives and needs that limit abilities to conform. On the contrary, power politics assumes that individuals and identity groups can be made to conform with institutional requirements.

Conflict resolution, being holistic, seeks to analyze not merely social requirements for the individual to conform with social norms, but also the need for institutional norms to serve the interests of the person. The source of conflict is frequently, perhaps usually, the failure of institutions and power elite norms to adjust to human needs.

The term behavioral, therefore, takes on an extended meaning: it is not just how people behave, but why they behave as they do and the constraints imposed on inherent genetic attributes. See **Compliance** and **Human Needs**.

C

Caucusing. A *caucus* is a closed meeting of members of a political party or a small group within a party that discusses tactics. Within a negotiation and mediation frame the term is sometimes used to describe processes in which the mediator has discussions with parties separately, exploring possibilities of compromise.

It is not a term used in conflict resolution in which processes require face-to-face facilitated discussion between parties to a conflict. On the contrary, caucusing or any separate discussion between a party and the facilitator would destroy the neutrality of the facilitation process, and prejudice, also, the analytical process by which the parties are led to redefine relationships and make an accurate costing of their policies.

Compliance. *Compliance* is a term suggesting a disposition to yield to others, and especially to a society and its social norms. It carries with it an assumption that individual behavior is wholly malleable. Antisocial behaviors, protest movements, and rebellions are, by implication, avoidable behaviors and, therefore, subject to law enforcement controls.

The conflict resolution or problem-solving frame has emerged because the evidence is that this notion of compliance is too limited. There is required a recognition that in certain social or institutional circumstances non-compliant behavior is inevitable. Empirical evidence and recent theories of human needs now suggest that there are inherent human requirements that will be pursued by the person or the identity group regardless of consequences. These are needs perhaps more deeply ingrained than needs for food and shelter, and their pursuit can lead to deliberate self-sacrifice. Independence movements lead to wars in which great powers are defeated. Youth unemployment can lead to antisocial means of achieving identity. To the extent that there is a power of human needs, law and order, which attempts to impose unacceptable behaviors by coercive means, promotes conflict and violence.

Compromise. *Compromise* implies making concessions, perhaps a settlement of a dispute by mediation, or a middle position. But "conflicts" are defined as those situations in which no compromise is possible. Compromise is, therefore, not a term that is relevant to conflict resolution.

Conciliation. *Conciliation* means winning over an opposition by making friendly overtures. It is an essential part of social relationships, especially in situations in which there is no dispute that requires compromise and no conflict that might require fundamental changes in relationships. If it has an application to disputes and conflicts it would be in relation to gestures at a final stage of settlement or resolution.

Conflict. Struggles between opposing forces take many forms. *Conflict* has been used to include struggles that are over resources, ideas, values, wishes and deep-seated needs.

The emergence of conflict resolution as a process and a political philosophy requires a separation between situations in which there can be compliance and those in which such accommodation is not possible. For this reason a sharp distinction is made between disputes and conflicts. Conflicts are struggles between opposing forces, struggles with institutions, that involve inherent human needs in respect of which there can be limited or no compliance, there being no unlimited malleability to make this possible. See **Identity** and **Recognition**.

Consensus. The notion of widespread agreement in traditional power terms carries with it the implication that those who are not in agreement should accept the majority view. This is the essence of the notion of democracy. It follows that there are those who have a right to expect obedience, and others who have an obligation to obey. This suits well the administration of societies in which there are privileged and underprivileged, ethnic minorities, and others who are not part of the consensus.

Within a conflict resolution frame *consensus* has the implication of consent by those who are not part of the majority accepted group. This probably requires processes that are nonadversarial and problem solving, as distinct from adversarial political party and industrial processes. It is this problem with consensus as the basis of systems that makes necessary conflict resolution as a political philosophy.

Consent.   *Consent* means giving assent, implying harmony of opinion in public policy making. Democracies operate on the basis of majority support for leaders and policies. But within adversarial party political systems such majority support frequently lacks harmony of opinion. Substantial minorities may be adversely affected without their consent. A financial policy decision may have widespread support, but it may create youth unemployment without their consent. Conflict resolution seeks to bridge the gap between harmony of opinion and consent by introducing nonadversarial problem-solving processes that involve all who are affected by policies. This implies bottom-up decision-making processes. See **Consensus**.

Costing.   Estimating the costs and consequences of a policy or specific action is a usual process in decision making. (See **Decision Making**.) When, however, *costing* includes likely responses from others, precision is not possible, at least in the absence of some interactive process through which responses can be determined.

In a power or bargaining frame such interactions are not possible. Talking to the enemy is a sign of weakness, as is revealing underlying reasons for policies. It is only when there is some facilitated analytical process that there can be a reliable costing of policies. In conflict resolution costing takes on an analytical meaning.

Culture.   The total range of activities and ideas of a people includes their means of dealing with disputes and conflicts. The implication is that dispute settlement and conflict resolution processes are cultural. It is power processes that seem to be most widely observed, probably for reasons of evolutionary experiences common to all peoples. It is sometimes argued, therefore, that the introduction of problem solving processes in one culture, or into United Nations programs, would not make them relevant for other cultures. In practice this would mean that no processes except power bargaining are relevant in any conflict that cuts across cultures.

Conflict resolution has a focus on frustrated human needs. Such needs are a part of human inheritance and common to all peoples, regardless of culture. It must be assumed, therefore, that analytical processes, which seek to reveal those needs that are held in common, are applicable to all peoples in all cultures. Although there may be different cultural means of dealing with disputes, which themselves take different forms in different cultures, analytical problem-solving processes that seek to get to the source of conflicts have a universal relevance.

D

Decision making. In a power frame *decision making* is a reactive process not far removed from reflex actions. There is stimulus and response. Even more thoughtful decision making within a power frame remains reactive in the sense that the response is only to a perceived situation with no certainty of accuracy. The assumption is that, with adequate power, decisions can be enforced regardless of response. Adequate power, however, cannot be determined until the total situation is assessed, which is not possible when decision making is reactive. Authoritative parents often misjudge responses. Countries often lose wars they initiate.

An interactive or costing frame (see **Costing**) is one in which parties analyze their decision making assumptions by interaction with parties affected before a final decision is taken. In theory, within such a frame no party to a conflict would enter into a war and lose it, or even win the war and lose the peace. Interactive decision making is the key, not only to conflict resolution, but also to conflict provention. (See **Provention**)

Decision making has tended to become more and more centralized within the nation-state system of government. In getting to the sources of problems, however, it is necessary for decision making to be from the bottom up. It is at the local level that the nature of problems can be identified and dealt with. Conflict resolution as a political philosophy implies a great deal of bottom-up decision making, with authorities at higher levels having a coordinating role.

There is an extensive literature on decision making, but almost all is within the traditional power frame. Conflict resolution as a study is clearly within the decision making field. It touches on management studies and challenges the traditional employer-employee adversarial nature of management decision making. It also challenges legal decision making, which is largely based on precedent, and frequently lacks consideration in the particular case of human behavioral considerations.

Deep-rooted. Deep-rooted is the term used in conflict resolution to apply to the inherent human needs that are associated with conflicts, human needs that cannot be compromised, as distinguished from the negotiable interests associated with disputes. The term is intended to imply an inability to conform, an absence of malleability, when there are certain human needs involved.

Dehumanize. Typically in dispute and conflict situations the parties involved *dehumanize* each other. The "other" is not "us" and, therefore, has different values and motives. This makes possible interpretations of behaviors that fit explanations of events, even though far removed from behavioral realities. Facilitated conflict resolution processes seek to help parties redefine relationships by questioning the assumptions each side is making about the perceptions and motivations of the other. Once all parties redefine relationships by reference to shared human motivations, for example in a case in which separate autonomies might be sought, there is understanding of positions and viable options can be explored.

Democracy. In early utopian thinking the power elite had at its disposal the armed forces, administration, and resources to ensure the security of those who claimed the right to govern. Forms of government evolved in due course that legitimized organized opposition to ruling elites, reflected in England in the formation of Houses of Commons and Lords. In due course the meaning of *democracy* became majority government. The word democracy is now widely used as the symbol of freedom, the ideal form of government. It, however, still tends to exclude minorities in the decision-making process and is characterized by the original adversarial political, legal, and industrial institutions: government and opposition facing each other in confrontational mode, prosecution and defense, management and workers.

Democracy takes on a new meaning in a problem-solving frame, especially when processes of interactive decision making are adopted at the political level. In the contemporary global society, in which minorities are seeking separate autonomies, in which ethnic and related identity conflicts are widespread, the majority government idea can no longer be justified. As yet there is no term that separates adversarial forms of democracy from problem-solving forms because within a power frame it is assumed that there is majority rule to which all should conform. The central authority has the duty to suppress dissident minorities. In the traditional power frame democracy means only majority support for policies. In a problem-solving frame there can only be "consent" or true "consensus" democracy, implying quite different decision-making processes. See **Consensus** and **Consent**.

Deterrence. Until the early 1960s there was no questioning of the proposition that *deterrence* deters. Foreign and domestic law-and-order policies were based on this assumption. Failures in deterrent strategies were attributed to inadeqate employment of threat and coercion. The empirical evidence (e.g. the defeat of great powers by small powers or persistent street violence in societies) and then some years later a theory suggesting that behavior was not wholly malleable, led to a questioning of this assumption. It is this realization that deterrence does not reliably deter that led to the consideration of options, and especially the analytical approach to specific situations of conflict and to conflict "provention" by appropriate changes in policies and in institutions. See **Provention**.

Dispute. An argument, debate, or quarrel is usually termed a *dispute* to differentiate it from a more serious confrontation that cannot be dealt with by compromise or fighting. It is settled by some form of power bargaining or by legal processes. The term does not carry any connotation that would suggest the nature or the source of the argument, whether it is over an idea, a property, or some aspects of a personal or institutional relationship. In a power frame, sources of disputes are of less importance than the settlement process outcomes.

In a problem-solving frame the sources of arguments are important. For this reason *dispute* is given a more precise meaning. It is confined to situations, usually involving material considerations, that are subject to negotiation and legal processes, and to compromise. *Conflict* is reserved for those confrontations that involve nonmalleable behaviors, requiring analysis of sources and remedies that address the behavioral institutional problems.

E

Ethics. All societies have their norms, including moral principles and sets of values. In the power-elite frame are the values that support existing institutions and norms. *Ethics* relates, therefore, to cultures.

If there were an acceptable behavioral explanation of conflicts that cut across cultures, then there could be universal norms and values. Ethics would take on a new meaning. The human needs frame, which is the basis of conflict resolution, provides that explanation. Ethics comes to mean behaviors that do not damage relationships based on individual self-esteem and identity, but, on the contrary, seek to enhance them.

Ethnic. *Ethnic* is a general term that covers various forms of identity groups: racial, cultural, religious, or some combination of these. Conflict resolution thinking confronts well-meaning and idealistic attitudes shared widely by more privileged sections of societies that advocate far greater assimilation. The human need for identity and the sense of security it gives, lead to a far more positive connotation.

There can probably be some movement away from security through ethnic groups toward greater assimilation by encouraging functional relationships among identity groups, leading in due course to the breaking down of identity boundaries. This, however, would require fundamental changes in institutions and social structures to bring about far greater equalities of opportunity and in living conditions.

F

Facilitation. Given problems in interactive decision making, especially within the context of power politics, there is obviously a need for a facilitator. This role should not be confused, however, with the role of the mediator in a dispute, who seeks an acceptable compromise. The role of the facilitator is to help parties define their conflict by getting to the behavioral elements that are usually suppressed or hidden in any power bargaining. *Facilitation* in this sense requires a new profession with specific education in the behavioral components of relationships, and in particular the nature of human needs and the ways in which they are pursued regardless of consequences, and specific training in bringing these to the surface.

The role of the facilitator is not confined to helping the parties to a conflict resolve their problem. It includes pointing out the wider social implications of any agreement. Parties immediately concerned can arrive at an agreement that could prejudice wider social relationships. It is relevant for a facilitator to enact this role because, ultimately, the parties directly concerned are also likely to be adversely affected by a short-sighted solution.

Fault. In a facilited conflict resolution process there is an emphasis on analysis. The presumption is that all parties involved are acting in what they perceive as their best interests. No party is guilty of any *fault* at least until an analysis is complete. Then *fault* is likely to be interpreted as a mistake in costing due to some misjudgment or misperception.

Fault is likely to be found in social structures that provoke certain behaviors rather than in behaviors themselves.

Functional. In dictionary terms, *functionalism* is a theory of design: the form of anything should be determined by its design purpose. *Functionalism* suggests agreements arrived at to promote shared purposes. There are many different ways of achieving a purpose. Cars can be driven on different sides of the road. It is convenient, functional, for all to agree on which side cars should be driven. There are international "functional" agreements that deal with navigation, air controls, trade practices, control of the international spread of diseases, and many others. Because they are in the interests of all, little enforcement is required.

G

Government. *Government* is the exercise of political authority over a people. It embodies all the concepts inherent in the notion of political power: the right to govern, the obligation to obey, and, at a deeper level, the malleability or ability of those governed to conform regardless of the behavioral conditions imposed.

In a problem-solving frame its meaning is far more linked with management, leaving open the possibilities of it being subject to consent by consent-building processes.

H

Holism. The tendency in the scientific age has been more and more toward specialization. Thinking was broken down into separate "disciplines" at the end of the last century, and now there is greater and greater specialization in every discipline. Few doctors seem to treat the body as a whole, frequently arriving at an inadequate diagnosis as a result. Many economists focus on some financial aspect of an economic problem, having little interest in wider social consequences.

Conflict resolution seeks to deal with problems of conflict and conflict provention by bringing together both behavioral and institutional influences, and each of these areas must be treated in a comprehensive way. It this sense it is introducing *holism* into political thinking. It becomes, as a consequence, a challenge to traditional disciplines.

Holism is not necessarily less "scientific" or reliable. On the contrary, though it may not be as statistical in its approach, its analysis of a total situation can be more reliable. This is because it is deductive, relying on adequate theories of behavior, rather than relying only on empirical data for its explanations and analyses.

Human Needs. It is the notion of *human needs* that separates power theories from conflict resolution theories. Traditionally it has been accepted that there are human needs for food and shelter, and that persons will struggle to have these needs satisfied, provided, of course, that there is sufficient food available to prevent a state of resignation.

The idea that there may be more fundamental human needs that are inherent, needs that will be pursued by any means available including the risk to life, has emerged only in recent decades. The power of human needs has helped to redefine power political thinking.

I

Identity. In a power frame, as for example in industrial relations, many persons have no separate *identity*. It is identity that provides the means of personal recognition and self-esteem. There probably cannot be harmonious social relationships in the absence of means of satisfying what may be an inherent human need for personal identity and recognition of the person in the context of meaningful groups. It is street gangs and conspicuous behaviors of many kinds that are a source of identity in the absence of socially acceptable means of acquiring a social role and personal identity.

An identity *group* is one in which individuals who share a particular characteristic, racial, ideological, national, or other, come together to promote or to defend their roles. Although belonging to such a group may limit individual identity and role, it is also a means of promoting that identity and role. The determination of identity groups to pursue their need for separate recognition and self-determination is proving to be a greater power than military or coercive force.

It is to be noted that it is the denial of individual identity within a society that leads to group identity, requiring group loyalty and, frequently, loyalty to a leader, a Hitler or some other, with all kinds of destructive policy consequences. It is in this way that domestic problems spill over into ethnic and international conflict. Peacekeeping and peacemaking do not address this human source of conflicts and, therefore, do not resolve a conflict.

Integration. In the power frame *integration* has an idealistic connotation. Integration by force, however, is a major source of conflict in the global system.

In a problem-solving frame, separation of ethnic groups could be positive in the sense that independence and the separate identity it provides can lead to functional forms of integration, thus integration could be achieved by initial disintegration.

Interests. *Interests* include hobbies, ideologies, and belief systems generally. Interests are also given the special meaning of possessions, properties, investments, and the organizations that can promote such material interests.

The significance of interests in a problem-solving frame is that, whereas material interests are usually negotiable, others tend to be associated with identity and are not negotiable. It is this difference between material interests and identity interests that is the basis of the distinction made between disputes and conflicts.

J

Justice. *Justice,* like *democracy* and many other terms widely used within a power frame, has a specific meaning within that frame. The application of law is described as justice. But, like democracy, it has this special meaning only within the system in which it exists. It becomes, therefore, a cultural term, meaning different things in different circumstances.

In a problem-solving frame *justice* can be given a universal meaning only insofar as it reflects the satisfaction of human needs, which are by definition universal. See the human need for **Identity** above, which in turn relates to natural justice, equality, fairness, and other such social conditions.

L

Leadership. In a power frame, *leadership* is revered. There are instances in which countries have gone to war seemingly to demonstrate the power of leadership and to win respect. Such leadership, being a scarce resource, also reflects a personal drive for recognition. History could be rewritten to show that leadership is a major source of conflict. Ethnic conflicts are frequently triggered by leadership ambitions.

In a problem-solving frame leadership becomes facilitation, the pulling together and exploration of different and opposing ideas, and the promotion of a deep analysis of any situation before policy is determined.

Legitimate. *Legitimate* is one of those adjectives the meaning of which rests on circumstances: behavior is legitimate if it conforms with acceptable standards. As with justice, certain social and legal norms are implicit in that which is legitimate. Unacceptable leadership can be legitimate if it is constitutional. It has, therefore, a cultural connotation. It also has a wider meaning: that which is correct or logical and reasonable thinking.

In a problem-solving frame, policies and behaviors are legitimate to the extent that they satisfy human aspirations and avoid problems that lead to conflict.

M

Malleability. Something that is *malleable* can be worked into shape by hammering or other means of pressure without being broken. A basic assumption in political thought throughout the ages has been that people can be influenced, pressured, or, if necessary, forced to conform with existing social and legal norms. This has been assumed to be the case at all social levels, from the family to the international. Recent experiences at all levels, however, shows that this is not so. Human nature is not infinitely adaptable. Identity and recognition issues are clearly not controlled by such coercion. Street battles and wars are being lost by authorities with overwhelming coercive powers. This is an emerging reality that is central to conflict resolution thinking. It was the realization that deterrence does not necessarily deter that triggered thinking in this area back in the 1960s.

Management. In a power frame all *management* is
the hierarchical exercise of control. This concept
still dominates in industry, but applies also to public administration. It is a direct outcome of history,
but has persisted because of the assumptions, such
as malleability, that have been inherited along with
limited concepts of democracy and government.

In a problem-solving frame, management, like
leadership, is the task of bringing together different
ideas and practices to achieve agreed upon goals.

Mediation. Before there was any distinction made
between disputes and conflicts, *mediation* had an
almost universal use in describing interventions
into relationships.

Mediation is an art. It varies greatly according
to the belief systems of the mediator. If, in fact, the
problem in relationships turns out to be a dispute,
mediation can be successful. But frequently mediation does not reveal hidden issues, and mediators
frequently do not have the training required to
bring these to the surface. What appears to be a
dispute can turn out to be a conflict and mediation
in these circumstances can be dysfunctional.

Morality. The quality of being moral relates closely
to, and is frequently defined as, conformity. It is a
concept, like "social conscience," "ethics," and
many others that are implied as being required
within a power frame.

Morality in a problem-solving frame relates to
the observance of human needs and conduct necessary to accommodate them.

Multiculturalism. *Multiculturalism* is a recently
introduced word to describe those situations where,
as a deliberate policy, peoples from many different
cultures have been accepted as migrants. It does not
cover situations where there are conflicts between

different cultures that were included in past colonial territories. These are referred to as *multiethnic* conflicts. Multiculturalism has a positive connotation, implying harmonious relationships within the one society. It is to be distinguished from *assimilation*, which implies the breaking down of cultural barriers, as is the case when migrants are limited in numbers, and, over time, possibly become a part of the indigenous society. Multiculturalism is still experimental and it may be that steps must be taken to encourage a greater degree of assimilation at least to the extent that these separate communities no longer identify primarily with the cultures they have left behind. Much must depend on living conditions and opportunities and these experiments are likely to lead to ethnic conflict if living conditions deteriorate.

Conflict resolution practices have been applied to multiethnic conflicts. Their application to multiculturalism is still to occur.

N

Needs. See **Human Needs**.

Nongovernmental Organizations.

Nongovernmental Organizations (NGOs) cover a wide field of international relations. There is no governmental body, other than the United Nations, to which parties to a conflict can go for assistance in resolving a conflict. The United Nations has peacekeeping and peacemaking capabilities, but having been established within a power politics frame, it has no conflict resolution capabilities. Probably it is only an NGO that could provide the necessary informal and off-the-record intervention by facilitators.

P

Panel. The facilitator in a conflict resolution process is frequently a *panel* so that many different aspects—political, economic, social, psychological—can be analysed. In an important case, such as an international conflict, the panel might consist of half a dozen facilitators, who will spend considerable time interacting among themselves.

Peace. Traditionally *peace* has had the limited meaning of the absence of war. It does not necessarily mean a harmonious relationship. It is a term usually avoided in conflict resolution thinking, though still widely used by people and organizations interested in promoting harmonious relationships.

Peacekeeping and Peacemaking. *Peacemaking* and *Peacekeeping* are terms introduced to describe activities by the United Nations in separating parties to conflicts (peacemaking) and in maintaining an absence of violence (peacekeeping). There is not implied any attempt to get to the roots of the problem and to find solutions.

Power. *Power* is the ability to do something. *Power Politics* is a term used to describe the use of military power or its threat, or a balance of power to maintain peace or the absence of war. But power does not necessarily imply the use of force or the threat of force. Indeed, it can mean the ability to resist military threats and the exercise of pressures even by nonviolent means.

In the conflict resolution literature there are references to the power of human needs, that is, the abilities and willingness of communities to maintain their independence despite military threats. Power has, therefore, a wider meaning to include nonmilitary, noncoercive abilities.

Prejudice. Opinions based on inadequate information or false beliefs are the usual feature of conflictual relationships. Dispute settlement processes, which seek to find compromises, are not usually geared to expose *prejudices*. This is, however, the first and main task of facilitation. Questioning of the parties by a facilitator, and their questioning of each other, are important parts of the early interactions in the conflict resolution process.

Prevention. To *prevent* is to keep from happening, perhaps by restraining. It implies the use of force or the threat of force. *Prevention* describes the use of more police in the street to stem crime and violence, or the maintenance of power balances and peacekeeping. See **Provention**.

Preventive Diplomacy. This is a phrase employed by the United Nations to suggest means of anticipating a conflict. It usually implies military intervention, but it could mean in some circumstances only the threat of force made in a diplomatic setting.

In conflict resolution it would imply a more analytical means of dealing with a problem and the removal of structural conditions that might promote conflict.

Problem Solving. *Problem Solving* was, until recently, a mathematical phrase: a problem was a statement requiring a solution. It was also used in relation to a puzzle requiring a solution. In a power context it is understandable that the term has not been needed. Social problems were not solved. They were dealt with by coercive means. With evidence of failed deterrence processes, it has come to be argued that social problems have to be dealt with at the source, and thereby resolved. Hence the phrase "problem-solving conflict resolution."

Process. *Process* describes the means employed in decision making to reach a goal. Conflict resolution has certain tested processes. But as used in conflict resolution the term has a wider meaning. Anticipating conflict, avoiding it before it occurs, and removing its sources require continuing institutional change. No revolutionary new system by itself can lead to a stable society. Continuing change as circumstances and knowledge suggest is process. In this sense conflict resolution is politically neutral: starting from the present, whatever it might be, there is continuing facilitated change as circumstances require.

Provention. So much has power thinking dominated language that there is no word which suggests avoiding a problem or conflict by dealing with its sources. The focus has been on coercive or deterrent processes by which to prevent. (See above **Preventive Diplomacy**.) It has been felt necessary, therefore, to introduce a word especially for this purpose. *Provention* seemed to be appropriate. It refers to the means by which a situation is anticipated and dealt with by removing the possible causes of a conflict, with no reserve threat of force. It could mean secession if parties sought this, far-reaching economic policies, or whatever combination of policies might be required to make conflict irrelevant. In this sense provention could be a political philosophy, a general approach to government.

R

Race. In the postcolonial era in which independence movements are a major feature, more precision is required in the use of terms such as *ethnicity*, *tribalism*, and *race*. *Ethnic* is widely used to suggest differences ranging from religious to linguistic to physical characteristics. *Race* is usually more limited and confined to physical differences due to ancestry. These differences, however, are frequently minor and *race* may not be appropriate. Because *tribal* is associated with early societies there is a reluctance to use the term to apply to contemporary societies. But frequently this is a more appropriate term than *race* when describing contemporary conflicts. See **Ethnic**.

Recognition. A behavioral approach to conflict resolution, that is, getting to the sources of problems, has a focus on the inherent needs of the person and identity group. In the present state of knowledge this is a focus in particular on identity or social role, and *recognition* of this personal identity, together with some degree of security or continuity of this recognition. *Recognition* is given an altered meaning in conflict resolution in the sense that it is not applied just to acknowledge role or status in the particular case, which is the usual meaning, but is a required social condition to be applied to all members of a society. It is recognition of the person or the identity group to which the person belongs. It is not just a human right. It is a human need, and failure by societies to give this recognition leads to the use of any means available to acquire it, such as joining a street gang.

Reentry. The conflict resolution process is deeply analytical, leading to altered perspectives, radical changes in understandings of the points of view and motivations of the other party, and consideration of options not previously entertained. The parties are frequently represented by nominees of leaders, communities, or organizations in conflict. The nominees, having experienced this face-to-face analytical process, and having altered, sometimes fundamentally, their definition of the situation, face a major problem of *reentry* when they report back to those whom they represent, who have not had this experience. The facilitator constantly reminds participants of this problem, encouraging them to keep in close and continuing contact with their principals.

Resolution. Resolution within a power frame has the connotation of determination or firmness. Resolving has the connotation of bringing an argument to an end. Conflict resolution has a quite different meaning. It implies problem solving by deeply analytical means. No element of coercion is implied. The implication is that all parties to the conflict freely agree once they have redefined and reperceived relationships, and once they have done their costing, that is, once they have examined and taken into account all the relevant elements of relationships.

Right/Wrong. Within a power or a legal frame the notions of right and wrong prevail. The concepts relate to morality. As they reflect legal norms they must be treated as cultural. In an analytical frame what is right and wrong can be determined only after the reasons for the apparent antisocial behaviors are determined. Typically, when parties to a conflict are brought together, facilitators have their own preconceived beliefs, but, no less typically, they find themselves altering their perceptions as the sources of the conflict are revealed. If party A is responsible for circumstances that are unacceptable to party B, and B responds by nonlegal behaviors, it is dysfunctional to attribute wrong to party B.

Rights. *Rights* implies treatment consistent with justice or orderly arrangements. It is, therefore, a cultural term. Rights in one society may not apply in others. In recent years *human rights* has been used to suggest certain rights that cut across cultural boundaries, for example, rights of free speech and free association. But these are extensions made within the traditional power frame. They are the rights that more powerful states, with particular economic and political systems, would like to see others observing, thereby giving them strategic and trading opportunities.

Conflict resolution is concerned, not with the observation of certain rights, but with human needs that are common to all peoples. There has been for a long time an interest in the needs of people, ranging from basic needs of food, clothing, and shelter to psychological and social needs. It is important, therefore, to make a clear distinction between rights and needs. See **Human Needs**.

S

Security. *Security* is the state of being secure, including freedom from poverty, from theft, and from invasions of any kind. Its general political use is in reference to military security.

In conflict resolution the term is intended to signify the guarantee of the satisfaction of human needs, now and in the future.

Settlement. Disputes are *settled* by mediation and related processes. It is a term well within the power frame of thought. Conflict resolution avoids the term because of implications of bargaining. See **Resolution**.

Spillover. Many conflicts, especially at the international level but also generally, are a *spillover* of some internal institutional or personal problem. A head-of-state facing a critical domestic situation tends to divert attention to an external problem. In management, internal problems are frequently attributed to unrelated issues that are then dealt with as a diversion. The notion of spillover, leading to a search for sources of conflicts, is an important one in conflict resolution processes.

Sponsor. *Sponsor* refers to the person or organization taking the initiative in bringing together parties to a conflict. It is most unlikely that a party to a conflict will approach the other side with the suggestion of informal and analytical discussions, even facilitated ones. This would be interpreted as weakness within a power negotiating frame. At best one party might make a challenge to the other, probably a public one. Similarly, it is unlikely that a party would approach an NGO or a person with a suggestion of facilitating discussion. The initiative must come from a person or organization willing to provide facilitation. The role of sponsor is an important one, and there are important rules to observe (see the chapter on Conflict Resolution Processes).

Structural Violence. *Structural Violence* was a term introduced in the 1960s to direct attention to the way in which institutions and policies damage or destroy individual values and development. The absence of employment or a social role, the lack of opportunities for education and development, are examples of structural violence. Structural violence is probably the major source of crime and aggression in societies, which is why problem solving conflict resolution seeks to move beyond a particular situation and to enter the field of political philosophy.

T

Third Party. The *third party* is the facilitator or panel of facilitators. The term is used even though there may be more than two parties in conflict present at a facilitation.

Tribal. See **Ethnic** and **Race**.

V

Values. The term *values* seeks to describe those thoughts and attitudes that are considered desirable by a society. It is another cultural term unless the context is the observation of human needs that are universal. Conflict resolution processes seek to reveal to opposing parties the way in which they have failed to recognize shared values, as for example, values attached to independence or effective political participation. In this way, what was perceived as a threat is reperceived as an understandable response to given circumstances, and adjustments can be made.

Violence.   See **Structural Violence**.

4

Conflict Resolution Processes

The intervention of a third party into relationships between others is a delicate task and can easily do more harm than good, especially when the relationships touch upon deeply felt issues, as is the case with conflicts. Interventions into conflictual relationships by persons who do not have the necessary knowledge and skills, perhaps using management or mediation skills, must be regarded as dysfunctional behavior, as unethical as pursuing a medical or any other professional calling without the necessary qualifications.

In dispute mediation there can be a degree of flexibility without the possibility of causing permanent damage; but not so in the case of conflicts. There is no room for pragmatism and expediency.

In all social relationships, as in all games, there have to be rules so the participants can fruitfully interact with each other. Everyone then knows what is expected and how to respond. It would be impossible to play a game if the rules were subject to alteration or modification ad lib. In analytical facilitated conflict resolution, where tight control of discussion is required, it is most important that the rules are clearly understood, consistently observed by the facilitators, and respected by all concerned.

If rules were interpreted merely as guidelines, they might be ignored or applied differently according to the pressures of circumstances. However, the delicate nature of facilitated interactions between parties to a conflict requires the application of tested procedures and does not allow for innovations except as a result of careful prior consideration.

Rules must be deduced from, and be in accord with the theoretical framework of conflict resolution. Their precise nature also emerges out of experience. Although the evolution of theory and experience with the process will lead to changes in the rules, departing from them for reasons of temporary expediency is risky and cannot be justified.

For example, when the sponsor is speaking about the process with the leading representative of a party to a conflict and asking for nomination of participants, the sponsor may be tempted into a discussion of some aspect of the conflict. This could prejudice the neutral role of the facilitator provided by the sponsor. To take another example, the panel may be tempted *not* to intervene when participants stray from the current agenda item and start discussing proposals before the analysis is complete. Experience has shown that this can derail the whole process.

There have been examples of persons intervening in ethnic and international conflicts who have engaged in discussions with parties separately. Those working in the field of dispute settlement frequently favor such caucusing. This has been traditional in industrial relations and is often practiced in matrimonial counseling. The attempt is to find how far one party is prepared to compromise and adjust to the other.

Although caucusing could be useful in a management or interest bargaining situation, it destroys the neutrality credibility of a third party in a tense situation of serious conflict. Even at tea breaks, discussion between facilitators and one of the parties alone is discouraged. More important, caucusing would destroy the central purpose of the facilitated process, that is, to reveal to each party by direct dialogue the attitudes and motivations of the other, and the costs of various policy options.

Another rule is confidentiality. The process is an analytical one. As is the case with personal counseling, confidentiality is a basic requirement. This is not just an issue of professional ethics. It is a practical one also. Parties in conflict, especially at a political level, cannot afford to be seen talking to the "enemy," or be perceived as weak and prepared to alter positions. If publicity were associated with the process there would be few who would be attracted to it, and little shift in positions by any who took part.

Many who intervene in conflict situations like to be conciliatory, and, therefore, pragmatic, especially when the analysis is found to be upsetting or when it provokes hostile responses, which is frequently the case at an early stage. But this destroys the process. As is the case with psychoanalysis, searching questions must be pursued. Emotional reactions must be expected and respected, but not avoided.

As in the case with the language of conflict resolution, a study of these rules gives insights into the nature of conflict resolution and its processes.

Conflicts have been defined as problems resulting from threats to or deprivations of the basic human needs of peoples of all ages and all cultures. Accordingly, these rules have been drafted to apply to conflicts at all social levels, from children and parents to relationships between nations. The rules set out below include those required at high levels, international, multiethnic, industrial, and others, where there are leaders to be contacted and who would nominate representatives. Clearly, some will not apply when individuals or small groups are interacting directly. Others will not apply in the absence of a facilitator. But the principles implied even in seemingly irrelevant rules will be clear and can be applied appropriately in all circumstances.

It will be seen that these rules have a wider social relevance than merely the resolution of particular conflicts. They point the way toward the education of parents, and the preschool education of children through to education at higher levels and in relationships generally. The common theme is respect for and preservation of individual identity, and, therefore, administrative and social norms that involve individual participation in decision making.

Further extensions become self-evident. It follows that if social norms are not observed there is a presumption that the person concerned is experiencing or has experienced in the past a denial of identity, perhaps through parental behavior, perhaps through unemployment or the absence of a social role. The relevant remedy in such cases is not punishment, which could only make the condition worse, but an adjustment of the environment and help in regaining a sense of identity.

Currently in some countries there are attempts being made to bring criminals and their victims together, in the presence of a third party, so that the victims can receive explanations and feel that justice has been done, and so that the guilty can perceive the human effects of their crimes. Such a process needs to be extended to include processes of analysis that would help also to explain the reasons for the crime, and thus be of even more benefit to the victim as well as fostering the adjustment of the criminal.

Parties that are engaged in ethnic conflicts typically commit the same kind of atrocities while accusing each other of their crimes. In a facilitated interaction the underlying prejudices and fears can be brought to the surface, and the shared circumstances of resource scarcities, leadership rivalries, and others, dealt with. In many cases of ethnic conflict ethnicity itself will be found not to be the source of the problem.

In practice one of the most relevant applications of these rules is at a community level where social problems occur. More police in the streets cannot make any significant long-term contribution to the widespread problems of burglaries, sexual abuse in the home, school absentees, drugs, and so on. Community organizations that involve all members in one way or another, and the local activities of appropriately trained social workers, would be far more relevant.

Conflict resolution processes are designed to deal with specific problems, as indicated above. But once the issues approach the broad policy level, the processes become an alternative to the traditional adversarial party power politics, thus becoming the basis of a political system.

The difference in process has its implications for policy content. For example, financial and economic policies have been based on the goal of improved development by investment, leading to an increase in Gross National Product (GNP). In practice this is an extension of the elite controls associated with Western style democracies where there are unrepresented peoples and their neglected interests. The longer term consequences are an alienated 20 per cent or so of populations and a great deal of social disruption by crime and violence. A problem-solving approach that took into account the interests of all concerned, including the interests of future generations, would be directed towards policies that put quality of life (QOL) before GNP.

The rules set out in the next chapter are under various headings, commencing with "Rules of Sponsorship," and working through to the actual processes.

5

The Processes of Conflict Resolution

The Rules of Sponsorship

The first rules relate to the role of the sponsor, that is, the person or institution which initiates and pursues the facilitated conflict resolution process.

> **Rule One.** A sponsor should not approach parties to a dispute with a view to facilitating a resolution unless the sponsor can provide facilitators who possess the required training and skills.

Conflict situations are often costly in lives and in resources; people involved are desperate and have high expectations for an intervention of this kind. Unless there can be adequate follow-through, and the ability to sustain the project over an extended period of time, interventions should not be attempted.

> **Rule Two.** A sponsor should not approach parties to a conflict without being sure it is possible to stay with the situation until the services offered are no longer required.

The sponsor's first step in working with a given conflict situation is to identify the parties involved so appropriate approaches can be made to their leaders or decision makers.

This is usually not a simple task. Indeed, sponsors are likely to have to adjust their perceptions as they proceed. A simple and atypical case is one in which there are only two parties and the issues can be defined clearly. In these cases, identifying the parties presents few problems. In the more typical case there will be many parties and issues, and, when a conflict has been protracted, there will be many subparties. This occurs in continuing industrial and communal conflicts. The protracted nature of a conflict tends to lead to divisions within each party and to the emergence of rival leadership groups.

In these circumstances a comprehensive list needs to be made of parties and issues, set out, insofar as is possible, in an order that reflects the degree of each party's involvement in the conflict. For example, in a conflict in which the parties each have external backing, the resolution process should begin with those whose transactions are most affected, not with the external parties, even though they may appear to be more influential.

Conflict resolution will not be complete until all parties and issues on this list have been brought into the resolution process. The list may be amended as further insights into the nature of the conflict require.

> **Rule Three.** At the outset, the first task of a sponsor is to identify, as far as is possible, the parties and issues relevant to the conflict, and their degrees of involvement. This task is to be accomplished prior to initiating any approaches.

The facilitated conflict resolution process, being intensely analytical by nature, must be limited in regard both to parties and to issues. The parties to a complex conflict are not all brought in together. The problem-solving process requires the separate treatment, that is, separate facilitated discussions, of those issues that relate to particular parties. However, such separate treatment must be carried out in the context of the whole situation. The discovery of options at one level enables movement of the process to more peripheral levels.

In all conflicts there are those who are immediately concerned and others who have interests in the conflict and its outcome. In industrial relations there are those immediately concerned within the company affected, and unions and other interest groups that might be affected by outcomes. In an ethnicity conflict that has wider strategic implications, the resolution of the conflict between the parties immediately concerned tends to be treated by external parties as less important than its control, which may occur through coercive means, within some great power strategic plan. In the longer term this approach is self-defeating as it leads to protracted, though perhaps submerged, conflicts, evidenced by terrorism and other means of protest.

The tendency in traditional conflict settlement procedures is for the more powerful parties to be brought into discussion and for them to deal first with the issues that are relevant to them. This approach frequently pushes aside the central sources of the conflict. Facilitated conflict resolution seeks to begin with the core issues and the parties directly concerned with them.

> **Rule Four.** The starting point in the analysis and resolution of any conflict is where the closest relationships have broken down, that is, within parties or between communities within a state. The analysis then moves outward until all parties and issues are dealt with.

We have been looking at the problem of parties and issues from the perspective of an ideal institutionalized system in which a large number of facilitators are available and have adequate resources at their disposal. Typically sponsors who have limited resources at their disposal are forced to concentrate at any one time on a few parties and to deal only with the issues that involve them. For this reason it is important that the sponsors keep the remaining parties informed of their planning.

> **Rule Five.** If the sponsor is not in a position to organize more than one seminar series at a time, a list of parties and issues (with some indication of the order in which they will be addressed) should be communicated to all parties. The communication

should clearly point out that no discovered option that affects others will be implemented until there is discussion of it with all concerned.

Entry Rules

The traditional and normative approaches to conflict resolution via courts, adjudication, or binding mediation, have often been rejected. Parties to conflicts, as distinct from disputes, are not prepared to let third parties make decisions on their needs and values. Recent innovations such as shuttle diplomacy have also failed because there is no direct interaction and, therefore, no means for the parties to analyze the problem. There are, consequently, no acceptable institutionalized processes available to parties in dispute, nor are such parties aware of any acceptable alternatives. As a consequence, serious conflicts are not being resolved.

The notion of problem solving means leaving decision making in the hands of the parties until an agreement is reached that satisfies the needs of all concerned. It also involves the separate conceptualization of needs and interests. It is based on the theory that common or universal needs of both sides can be met, and that, in this sense, a "win-win" outcome is possible. These ideas are all outside the traditional conceptual framework of decision makers who conceive of relationships as based on relative power and who hold that direct discussion with an "enemy" is treason. The entry problem for a sponsor of facilitated conflict resolution is, therefore, a difficult one.

Even though the parties to a dispute may be aware of this problem-solving approach, they may hesitate to seek assistance for fear that the rival party would interpret this act as an admission of weakness. This applies to all levels of interaction. For this reason, at least until there is some change in conventional wisdom or some introduction of institutionalized processes, the sponsor must make the initial approaches to parties in conflicts and should not expect to be approached. Moreover, the sponsor must make the approaches to both parties simultaneously so that both can respond without an appearance of weakness.

At the international level the most effective method is to approach heads of government or leadership of communities directly since it is their interest in and knowledge of the process that are finally important. Experience has shown that heads of state and communities often respond positively and quickly to the idea of exploratory discussions for which they do not have to take any public responsibility. It is usually necessary to set out the approach in writing, to invite participation in the same form and simultaneously to all parties, and to follow up with personal visits. If such a direct approach is not possible it is often practical to take advantage of available contacts.

In industrial, community, small group, and personal conflicts, entry may be through professional associations, attorneys, social workers, and others who are aware of the need in particular cases for assistance they are not in a position to provide.

Rule Six. All communications to parties should be directly to those involved, and in the cases of large groups, at a leadership or near-leadership level, or at least with the knowledge of leadership.

It is most important that sponsors are, are seen to be, and remain neutral. Neutrality does not imply absence of sympathy. The fact that the sponsor wants to deal with a conflict situation, and the sponsor's ability to identify with the parties concerned, however, can readily be misinterpreted by parties as favoritism. Care must be taken to avoid this impression.

Rule Seven. Communications should be simultaneous and identical with no issues raised in invitations. Follow-up visits in support of invitations should be confined to a description of the processes and detailed arrangements.

In the case of large groups, such as nations, the parties are invited to nominate representatives who are one-removed from decision makers, for example, members of parliament, personal friends in whom there is confidence, and others. The possibility of failure will then be of less political concern and there cannot be complaints about talking with the enemy. (In many cases parties to conflicts do not "recognize" each other or are at war and, therefore, cannot be seen to be involved in any direct way.) Often scholars selected by leaders can represent a party well in initial meetings because of the analytical nature of the process. An additional advantage of meetings of scholars is that the unofficial and research nature of the process is emphasized, and this is more acceptable to political leaders.

> **Rule Eight.** Parties should be invited to send participants who are not official representatives, but who have easy access to decision makers.

It is necessary for factions within parties to be represented to ensure successful reentry. An option discovered will not be viable unless opposition groups support it, and this will not happen unless they have been involved. Inevitably, including rival political party representatives on a team causes some difficulties since they are, especially in party parliamentary systems of government, often reluctant to help the governing party resolve a problem. This is a challenge to the sponsor and facilitator, but must not be avoided. The participation of oppositions within a ruling political party, or others whose support for agreed proposals would be required, is also important because hard-liners have to be convinced. Their involvement at an early stage helps both in the analysis of the situation and in the reentry.

> **Rule Nine.** The participation of all factions within a party should be sought.

The Third Party

The fact that the facilitated process is an analytical one requires that the parties concerned can come together to examine each other's underlying motivations and goals in a direct interactive way. It must also allow them to define issues and make reliable assessments of the costs of their positions regardless of whether the parties are nations, communities, small groups or individuals, or a community and a central authority.

This process is in contradistinction to traditional practices in which the third party tends to consult separately with those involved in a dispute. It is clearly at variance with traditional diplomatic practices, in which relations are severed at times of high tension and conflict and in which governments operate through "protecting powers." This has been the handicap for mediators who move to and fro between parties. Hence the next rule is indispensible for facilitated conflict resolution.

Rule Ten. Parties to disputes must be placed in a direct analytical and nonbargaining dialogue.

The above rule implies the likely failure of processes involving direct bargaining from predetermined positions, or mediation or other processes that rely upon a third party to put forward proposals or to apply normative considerations. Yet direct interaction clearly requires the presence of a third party to offset any tendency for contending parties to see only that which they expect to see and to prevent them from lapsing into bargaining or adversarial interaction. In advising parties, sponsors should emphasize the need for a third party in any situation of tension, and should discourage direct interactions during the facilitation process.

Rule Eleven. A third party should be present in any dialogue among conflicting parties who are seeking to understand their conflict and to find an agreeable resolution.

The role of a third party is not to mediate in the sense of suggesting seemingly reasonable compromises. The third party role is to facilitate in the ways suggested above. There can be a settlement of a dispute by the use of superior power, or by an enforced ruling from a court. Resolution, however, implies the satisfaction of all non-negotiable values, leading to an outcome that does not require enforcement.

The current consensus view is that compromise is the best possible outcome of a dispute. However, in facilitated resolution of serious conflicts, compromise must be avoided because the issues being discussed are ones on which there cannot be compromise: identity, security, recognition, and others to which reference has already been made. There may have to be compromise on interests, which can be made the subject of some bargaining, but human needs, and sometimes cultural values, are not subject to compromise. Attempts to arrive at compromises are a reason for stalemates in negotiation. This is why a distinction must be made between goals and tactics. The goals cannot be compromised, but the means to reach the goals can. For example, possession of territory can be a tactic for attaining the goal of security. But security itself can best be secured by tactics that do not threaten or lessen the security of others. It is these considerations that are at the heart of conflict resolution processes. Conflict resolution hypothesizes that those issues that are at the basis of conflict, issues of human needs, do not involve scarce resources, but resources that increase with consumption. The more security (the goal, not the tactics to obtain security like the possession of a strategic hill) one party experiences, the more security will be experienced by others.

> **Rule Twelve.** The role of the panel in conflict resolution is not to seek compromises. It is initially to facilitate analysis so that goals and tactics, interests, values, and needs can be clarified, and later, to help deduce possible outcomes on the basis of the analysis made.

The third party has a key function to ensure that neither it nor the participants are working on false basic hypotheses about the nature of the particular conflict under discussion. There will be preconceived notions drawn from the media and official statements. It must be discovered whether the conflict is due to aggressiveness and leadership problems, fundamental drives of identity, recognition and distributive justice, or confusion over needs and interests. The panel must ensure that the opposing parties have every opportunity to assess each other's motivations and accurately to determine for themselves the nature of their conflict.

To make this possible, panel members must know what questions to ask, how to distinguish tactics from goals, and how to encourage the parties to reveal their deep motivations, values, and intents. These tasks require panel members not merely to have a broad knowledge of their own speciality and of conflict theories, but also to be familiar with theories of functionalism, institutions, legitimacy, and such relevant topics. They must have a knowledge of the way in which the normative and power-coercive philosophy has evolved and must recognize its strengths and weaknesses. Further, they must understand the logical relationships between traditional assumptions based on the state as the unit of analysis and the deterrent or defensive strategies that these theories produce, since this is the conceptual framework in which parties to disputes will be arguing. Similarly, panel members must be informed fully of the alternative human needs approach, the problem-solving strategies that are its logical outcome, how it has evolved from traditional thought, and relevant interdisciplinary studies.

The quality of the outcome and the success or failure of the facilitation are directly related to the contribution the panel can make. This is the case whether the panel is helping in the analysis of the conflict or helping the participants to think through their problems and arrive at outcomes that meet their needs. It is in this way that facilitation differs from the more passive role of "good offices."

Rule Thirteen. Panel members should be drawn from several key disciplines, they should be widely informed of different approaches in their own fields, have an adequate knowledge of conflict theories, and be experienced in the facilitation process, so as to help the parties to arrive at an accurate definition of the situation under examination.

One perspective that is clearly important is the gender perspective, and it is important to have panels that comprise both sexes. Sometimes an ethnic or class perspective may be important.

Rule Fourteen. It is necessary to have balanced viewpoints and perspectives represented on the panel, including gender, and where relevant, ethnic and class perspectives.

In the final analysis the parties to a conflict are the real experts. The conflict is theirs, and they must determine its nature by their own analysis of it. The data, facts, and interpretations must come from the perceptions and experiences of the opposing parties, not from the panel. For this reason panel members must not be prejudiced by preconceived views based on so-called expert knowledge of local conditions, as may easily be the case if a panel member is exclusively a specialist in respect to that conflict. All persons who serve on the panel should have the capability of placing the particular conflict in the wider perspective of social relationships.

Rule Fifteen. The panel should not include persons who have made an exclusive speciality of the particular conflict being analyzed or of the region in which the conflict takes place.

From time to time in all areas of thought there are significant paradigm shifts. In the analysis and explanation of conflict a consensus could emerge in support of one particular philosophical approach. Such a consensus would make it seem unnecessary for different philosophies and disciplines to be taken into account by the panel. However, even within an approach wholly oriented towards one particular philosophy, the testing function remains an important one. In some conflict situations leadership roles may seem to play a dominant part. For example, it may appear that there is a clear struggle between two factions for political power for its own sake. The power struggle could be a sufficient explanation of the conflict, suggesting the need for some third-party intervention to control the violence. Within a problem-solving framework the primary purpose of the interaction would be to demonstrate the costs and consequences of leadership interests and to include them within the problem-solving process.

Rule Sixteen. Endeavors should be made to bridge the traditional explanations of power rivalries and problem-solving approaches by considering all and incorporating the relevant ones into the problem-solving process.

Panel members are likely to have different approaches, particularly if they come from different disciplines. They may have some difficulty in communicating with one another. Yet in their role as a panel they must work together to ensure that the right questions are asked at the right time, that the parties are not confused by different approaches, and that the testing and constructive analyses are followed through logically on the basis of an agreed-upon process.

Rule Seventeen. Panel members must prepare and confer before and during the seminar, even adjourning discussions for this purpose, so that they are always acting together and with mutual understanding.

In order to have a spread of disciplines and approaches, and yet keep the numbers small enough for group dynamics to operate, the ideal panel is composed of four or five members, with about ten participants who are involved in the dispute. This can present a problem, for panel members ideally should know each other well, interact well, be selfless in not wanting to intervene or to make presentations merely to enact a role, be prepared to spend the time necessary in preparation and follow up, and be present all of the time at seminar discussions. An ideal panel would be a team that worked together professionally.

However, it may be necessary to make use of scholars who are available only for a particular seminar series. It is most important that they be present continually, as any absences of or changes in panel members during a facilitation are disruptive.

> **Rule Eighteen.** Panelists must be selected, not only for their professionalism in facilitation, but also for their talents and abilities to work within a team, and even then, only if they can be available as and when required.

Sponsors and Decision Makers

In facilitation, where parties are groups or nations and must be represented by nominated participants, the initial contact is usually made with leaders, decision makers, or their advisers. There is an obligation on the sponsors to communicate back to these persons at each significant stage, for example, after a seminar series.

This will be done from their own perspectives by participants, but a report direct to decision makers maintains the link with the sponsor and the process. This link has a specific value. First, it is often necessary to interpret a final agreed-upon statement in the light of the total proceedings, to assess the value of subsequent meetings from a perspective that is not confined to one party, and to arrange subsequent meetings, perhaps with some different participants. Furthermore, a stage is reached at which there should be a transition from informal and exploratory discussions to official negotiations. It is for the sponsor to suggest when this stage is reached and to facilitate the transfer.

There is an important confidentiality issue involved in reports to decision makers. The participants have been invited to a private discussion. It should be communicated to participants that reports to those who nominated them should be made and the reasons for making them should be given. It may be the case that in the views of the participants the stage is not yet ripe for such reports, and the panel should take these views into consideration.

Rule Nineteen. Sponsors should make reports to the leadership of the parties involved after each workshop series, or at agreed-upon stages in the total process.

Once viable options have been discovered it may be desirable to negotiate details, and for this purpose to transfer the discussions to a more official level. If some participants represent minority views within a party to the conflict it may be appropriate at this stage to limit participation to those who represent the point of view of the formal decision makers. Participants from opposition leaderships or political parties, for example, may play a constructive role in defining the problem and exploring a solution, but may have divided loyalties that cause them to undermine the drafting of an agreement that could give credit to the current group leadership or political party in power.

In particular, it will be necessary to work out the transition that may be necessary from exploration of options with opposition members present, to a later stage when only the representatives of decision makers may be involved. This is a stage for considering tactics, rather than substance. In some cases the transition may be by holding informal discussions between officials nominated by leadership within the same facilitated unofficial and quasi-academic framework. In others it may be necessary to arrange for unofficial participants to be briefed on official views and to arrange a means of direct communication during seminar discussions.

Rule Twenty. Sponsors should give special consideration to the transition stage between the unofficial discussions (which sometimes include participants representing opposition leadership or parties) and the official negotiations, and take whatever steps are required to prepare for this even before viable options have emerged in the seminars.

This need for transition raises issues of publicity. The unofficial problem-solving process is understood to be confidential. Sometimes not even the existence of discussions is made public. The format can be perceived as an academic, exploratory exercise, having nothing to do with decision making. In some cases this academic image is particularly valuable. However, there are bound to be leaks, especially when oppositions are included. They may wish credit, they may wish to embarrass, or they may wish to push the group leaders or government further and quicker than the latter believe they can go.

Rule Twenty-one. The panel should seek from participants specific agreement on what, if any, publicity is desired and generally seek to avoid any dysfunctional consequences of publicity.

Preparatory Rules

Inevitably there are financial problems inherent in the process. For example, governments cannot be seen to be taking an active interest, which would be implied by financial support, in discussions with "the enemy" or the factions "in rebellion." Factions in rebellion usually do not have financial resources. Small groups within a labor union are not in a position to meet, as unions can, the costs involved in facilitated processes. Minorities generally are not in a position to take time off, to travel, to pay for accommodation and incidental expenses. Furthermore, the first meeting, as has been stated, has to be at the invitation of the sponsors. The result is that the sponsors may have to be prepared to meet all the expenses of at least the first meeting. There are preparation costs, including fares for the initial visits by sponsors, and the costs of documentation and research. During the seminars there are all manner of ancillary costs—participants phoning home, receptions, etc.

> **Rule Twenty-two.** Before approaches are made there should be adequate funds for a first meeting so there are no unnecessary anxieties and savings.

Once the process has been initiated and when the parties have had time to establish their own funding, they should be encouraged to meet all their own expenses. This adds to their commitment. However, in many cases, especially in relation to conflicts involving underdeveloped countries, the parties may not be in a position to raise the substantial funds required for travel and accommodation.

Even when parties do take responsibility for their own expenses, there will still be substantial costs for the sponsors—fares and accommodation for panel members, receptions, office expenditures, document preparation, and so on. Facilitation of conflict resolution, dealing with deep-rooted conflicts, is never likely to be a commercial process in which high fees can be charged to meet such expenses. This applies especially to the international arena where seminars must be outside the environment of the conflict. The nature of "second-track diplomacy," the fact that it must be unofficial and not appear to be part of any formal process, inhibits support from the governments of participants. Funding might come from agencies of governments not involved and from other sources, but the seminars will never be self-supporting.

> **Rule Twenty-three.** Participants should be encouraged to organize within their own communities and to contribute to their transport and accommodation costs after the first meeting.

Furthermore, experience shows that opportunities for "entry" occur suddenly and sometimes without more than a few days' warning. Sometimes it is necessary to make quick visits or frequent telephone calls to "enter."

Rule Twenty-four. Reserve funding is necessary so that opportunities are not missed.

Location is an important consideration for several different reasons. It is necessary to have a neutral meeting point. At the same time it must be one that enables communication among participants and with those who nominated them. It should be as convenient as possible to participants and facilitators. The cost factor also enters in.

Sometimes there are visa problems to take into account. This is one of the first matters to be negotiated by the sponsor after invitations are accepted. In general there are advantages in meeting outside the immediate region of the conflict, at least at early stages. At the stage at which there appears to be a framework of agreement it may be desirable, especially in a communal dispute, to meet at the location and involve more directly a wider selection of interested factions and those who will finally have to take over negotiations and support agreements.

Rule Twenty-five. The sponsor must reach agreement with those who are nominating participants on the location of the meeting place, a neutral environment being the main concern.

Accommodation raises some important issues. In some cases when parties are in violent conflict there are tensions when they meet, and it is less embarrassing for all concerned if they arrive and are accommodated separately. Even when this is not the case it is desirable that parties be accommodated separately to prevent interactions outside the facilitated structure of the workshop.

Rule Twenty-six. Parties should be met separately and housed separately if possible.

Seating can present some problems. Each situation has to be handled differently according to circumstances. For example, when participants are in a violent conflict and feel deeply about "atrocities," they have difficulty in being polite even over coffee. In the beginning they do not like to sit facing each other during discussions. Panel members must be in easy verbal contact with each other and so must members of each party. Usually it is convenient for the panel to be at its own table facing the participants. If there are only two parties involved then each party can have a table facing the other and the panel at an angle of 45 degrees, forming a triangle. This helps to ensure that communication is through the panel until the participants feel free to interact directly. It also enables the parties to be in a face-to-face dialogue when they are ready for it.

> **Rule Twenty-seven.** Thought needs to be given in advance to seating arrangements, and changes should be made if, for any reason, the group dynamics require this.

It will be noted that no seating is provided above for observers or recorders. The presence of any persons other than panel members is a constraint, and recording—except the notes taken by participants and the panel—inhibits the kind of interaction sought.

There is only one exception to this rule, and that is the presence, when it is really necessary, of an interpreter. Often translation can be effective by seating participants whose knowledge of the language being used is inadequate next to participants in the same party who have no problems with it. Formal interpreting can be disruptive of interaction and should be avoided if it is clear that there is no real problem.

There will be occasions when language is a symbol of identity and, at least at the outset and until the nonbargaining nature of the workshop is understood, it may be necessary to accept the use of formal interpreting.

When an interpreter is employed, it should be not merely a professional interpreter, but one who also knows the language of conflict resolution.

Rule Twenty-eight. There should not be any observers nor should there be any provision for recording, even though the parties express no objections. However, appropriate interpreters should be available as required.

At times there is a need for discussion within parties or within the panel during seminar sessions. Sometimes separate meeting places are required at short notice, for example, when there is disagreement among members of a group.

Rule Twenty-nine. There should be provision for small conference rooms near the main meeting room in which parties can each meet separately.

The aim of the facilitated discussion is to encourage direct interaction resulting in the greatest accuracy in interpretations of motivations and intentions. The environment needs to assist this in every way. Though there is certainly no need for luxury, a relaxed environment, with some sense of space and some degree of comfort, assists interaction during sessions that are often tense and always long.

Rule Thirty. The sponsor should ensure that the general environment of the meetings and the comfort of the participants contribute to the facilitated discussions.

Sometimes parties will be from different cultures and have difficulty with names. There will be introductions at the outset, but adequate reminders are necessary. Name tags on the person are not required and would not be worn after the first day. Place names are useful.

Rule Thirty-one. There should be lists circulated of participants and panel members, and clear name displays in front of each.

It is important that the participants understand the process. They should know what is expected of them before they meet, what kind of expositions will be required of them at the initial meeting, and generally what the rules are. Some information will have been conveyed in the invitation and the follow-up visit. But some clear indication in advance of what will take place at the first meeting is important.

If at the outset the relationships are such that the participants can meet together, a useful device is an informal dinner, held the evening before the commencement of the seminar discussions. On this occasion the history and nature of the process can be described. Only the participants and the panel would be present; outside visitors would be intruders in this confidential assembly. If it is not possible for the participants to meet before the opening session, then each party needs to be informed separately.

Rule Thirty-two. Parties should be prepared for the first meeting, know what is expected of them, be aware of the role that will be enacted by the panel, and generally be made to feel comfortable about the process.

The Analytical Stage

The workshops or seminars are meetings, four or five days in duration, that compose one stage or phase of discussion. There may be several seminar series conducted before the discovery of agreed-upon options. In addition, there are likely to be other seminars concerned with the details of potential official agreements. Before discussion at each of the stages, a few general observations on the process and on the rules should be elaborated.

During the seminar sessions no communication of substance should take place except across the table in front of the panel. Private communications on matters of substance—as occur in a bargaining or negotiating framework—are dysfunctional. All concerned should share any communication, observation, or interpretation. In a second or subsequent series of meetings, when participants know each other, this is sometimes difficult to control. Some participants try to pursue their own personal interests and proposals privately. Nonetheless, the panel should stress the need for open communication. This is the kind of observation that can be made at an introductory informal dinner, or perhaps at the introductory meeting at the beginning of the series.

It is particularly important for panel members not to communicate privately with participants. Participants naturally scrutinize relationships between panel members and participants from the other side. Though they themselves may try to communicate particular observations privately with panel members—frequently about how deceptive the other side is—they lose confidence in panel members if they observe them communicating with others.

It will be found convenient to have lunches and sometimes evening dinners together. They tend to be working sessions. It is desirable, therefore, if a round table can be found to accommodate everyone, for it assists in making conversation a group activity, rather than many separate conversations.

> **Rule Thirty-three.** Participants should be asked not to discuss matters of substance outside the conference room. Coffee breaks, lunches, and other social occasions should be so organized to discourage participants from communicating privately either with other participants or with panel members on matters of substance. Panel members should not communicate with participants separately except on a social basis.

One task of the panel is to ensure that participants do not alter significantly their own value systems and perceptions of the nature of the conflict as a result of the group dynamics and friendships that develop during the process. When they "reenter," they will have a problem conveying any new ideas to decision makers in a convincing way if this happens. They have to return with an option that meets the needs of their constituency, who have not undergone the facilitated experience, and they have to be in a position to sell it, not on the basis of some altered personal relationship or changed perception of the opposing party, but on the basis of the merits of the option discovered.

Rule Thirty-four. In its procedures and in its observations and advisements, the panel must keep in mind the reentry problem of the participants.

The panel operates as a team, throwing the ball to the player whose specialization or participation seems to be most relevant at the time. In a panel in which members know each other, have prepared adequately, and have had experience, there should be no need for a chairperson as such. The panel operates as the chair with members of the panel inviting comments by participants and intervening as and when appropriate.

There is, however, a need for a person who acts in the role of host or hostess. This person may or may not otherwise play an active role. This person calls the meeting to order, outlines the program, decides when breaks are needed, and deals with organizational matters. The host chairperson also observes participants and ensures that all participants are given the opportunity to express themselves during the intense discussions. Panel members focusing on some particular aspect are apt not to observe participants who are not taking an active part at the particular moment. However, panel members also need to observe participant responses for consideration later during panel consultation.

Rule Thirty-five. The panel acts as a unit in conducting the seminar, with one member acting as the host/hostess and formal chairperson.

The discussions are designed to be open, with the panel moving the discussion from a consideration of the situation as perceived by the parties when they arrive, through analysis of the situation and the values and goals sought, to the discovery of options. There is no formal agenda, but there is a clear understanding among the panel on successive steps.

Rule Thirty-six. The step-by-step progression from initial perceptions, through analysis of the situation, to evaluation of these perceptions and to finding an agreed-upon definition, to exploration of options that meet the needs of all, should be maintained. However, there should be no fixed agenda of either specific items or timing.

The panel must exercise tight control of the discussions among participants to ensure that the rules of procedure are observed. Sometimes panel members, accustomed to free-flowing academic seminar discussions and the exercise of a great deal of mutual tolerance, are reluctant to intervene and control in this way. However, in a facilitated conflict resolution situation such control is an essential part of the process. If exercised early and consistently there is less difficulty at later stages, when deep feelings are being vented.

Rule Thirty-seven. The panel asks the participants to observe certain rules of procedure and makes it clear that it is the role of the panel to ensure that these are observed, that this is part of the process, and that this control is necessary for the success of the discussions.

If analysis is to be successful it is important to prevent presentation and discussion of any particular proposal until analysis is complete. There may be participants who are sure they have the answers, and even though they are discouraged by the panel from putting forward proposals, they will present all their questions and comments in relation to them. The panel should seek to control this situation. It is this process that makes the analytical-facilitated discussion distinctively different from the bargaining and negotiating framework where there are usually rival proposals being discussed from the outset.

> **Rule Thirty-eight.** There should be no proposals put forward by any side until the analysis of the situation is complete and a definition of the situation is agreed upon.

After the participants have given their first presentations it is necessary to allow for questions of clarification. Such questions, however, can quickly get out of control and become point-making or debating questions. This possibility draws attention to the need for control of discussion by the panel, and to achieve this members must be mutually supportive. The facilitation process was once labeled "controlled communication" because of the constant need for panel members to enforce the rules of communication. If debate occurs at this stage the analytical process is threatened. If control seems impossible, as it sometimes is when levels of tension and suspicion are high, then it is better not to have questions of clarification until all presentations have been completed, and then only after a summary presentation that the panel makes when it feeds back to the participants the main points they have made.

> **Rule Thirty-nine.** The initial exposition should be heard without interruptions. Following this, only questions of clarification should be asked by participants.

The panel should tell participants that the opening statements should deal primarily with the *values* and *goals* at stake in the conflict, even though this suggestion will make little difference. Participants will usually deliver the standard type of initial exposition, for at this stage they will confuse values and goals with tactics and their immediate conflict objectives. However, the request from the panel puts participants on notice that the panel is focusing on values and goals. It should also be recognized that participants may not have thought deeply about these matters.

> **Rule Forty.** When the panel asks the participants to make their opening statements, they should ask them to focus on the values and goals at stake in the conflict situation.

After all the participants have made their opening statements, and after controlled questions of clarification, the panel will pose questions of clarification, especially in relation to values and goals. These subjects will have been touched on indirectly or by implication, rather than stated directly. The rest of the first day is usually spent on such clarifications.

> **Rule Forty-one.** The panel poses questions of clarification, especially in relation to values and goals.

At this stage the panel should have sufficient information to make some analysis of values and goals, shared and in conflict. At a private evening meeting the panel should then prepare a discussion paper for the next day.

> **Rule Forty-two.** The panel should prepare (overnight probably) a statement of what appear to be shared and unshared values for submission to the participants.

When the participants receive the discussion paper, they will maintain that they have been misunderstood and attempt to restate their views, and they will disagree over values that the panel has stated are not shared. At this stage, some real analysis begins and stated positions tend to be pushed aside. The participants will tend to address each other rather than the panel.

> **Rule Forty-three.** The panel should allow discussions that help to clarify values to proceed freely, while intervening constantly to ensure that the dialogue remains analytical and does not regress to point-scoring debating exchanges.

From this point on the subjects for discussion have to be decided more pragmatically. The values discussion may be the most revealing, but it will be found that the participants need a lot of help in understanding the expositions of the opposing side. There will be disbelief, hints of deception, and a high level of distrust when values are expressed in a way that does not accord with preconceived notions.

It is at this stage that the panel has an important professional role to play, for a great deal of psychology and political psychology becomes relevant. At this stage the panel should be prepared to play an academic role and place the particular dispute in the context of other disputes that have similar features. Panel members should also explain the significance of needs and values and how they differ from interests.

> **Rule Forty-four.** The panel should take the opportunity to communicate any relevant knowledge that will help the participants to interpret what is being said. The panel may refer to other cases of conflict, to research findings on perception, and to theories of behavior.

When the input from the panel is received, the participants will learn a great deal, adopt a different language, and employ new concepts, at least when the input from the panel is relevant. If it is not relevant, the participants will show boredom and restlessness. Incidentally, this is a learning opportunity for panel members also, providing valuable information on conflict. At this stage political philosophies, approaches, and theories of cooperation and conflict are put to the test. It is in this sense that the total process should be regarded and treated as a research project with each seminar series leading to refinements of theory and practice.

> **Rule Forty-five.** The panel must be sensitive to audience response for there will be viewpoints and theories that are quickly absorbed because of their relevance, and others that will provoke no response because they are deemed not to be relevant to experience.

During the clarifications of values and goals, several key issues will emerge that go to the heart of the conflict. These may include leadership problems, identity issues, fears for the preservation of cultural values, and others.

> **Rule Forty-six.** The panel should move the discussion to the key issues once there has been clarity of goals and values. They should ensure that all discussions be kept within the analytical framework that has been established.

At this stage the panel will be considering the main propositions to include in an agreed-upon conclusion. These propositions will be short statements based on issues and concerns and agreements that emerged during all of the discussions. Sometimes an interjection or a passing comment will contain a hint of some concern, which will indicate that a proposition should be explored. In preparation for the drafting of agreed propositions, and to structure discussion of the many issues on the table, it is useful for the panel to prepare general propositions for consideration. As these will be more explanatory than the short statements that will appear in a final statement, they will help the participants to articulate and explain the propositions that will be agreed upon finally. This practice is designed to reinforce the learning and understanding process, and to help the participants in their own exposition, thus preparing them for their "reentry."

Preparation of a list of proposals, really a summary in proposition form of all that has taken place, is a major task for the panel. It usually has to be accomplished overnight. The panel will have taken notes of discussions from their different perspectives, and their task now is to ensure that all viewpoints are covered. It is important to include propositions that seem to be in doubt, which may have been implied but not articulated, and others that may have been mentioned but passed over without discussion.

> **Rule Forty-seven.** The panel should prepare a statement of the general behavioral propositions that have emerged. This list will be discussed in great detail.

The end goal of the first seminar series can usually be no more than a short statement of propositions on values and goals, that is, a definition of the conflict. The discussion of special issues will have clarified the values even more. It will be found that even if there were more time (and four days is about the limit that is desirable before participants report back) it could not be employed usefully. There will be fatigue, some euphoria, and a sense that this is about as far as the discussion can go prior to reporting back.

> **Rule Forty-eight.** The panel should prepare a draft statement of agreed-upon propositions. It should be submitted to the participants when the panel feels they are ready to give it their detailed consideration.

The Search for Options

Whether it be at the first seminar series (which is unlikely) or at a second some weeks later after discussions back home, the next step is for facilitated discussion in which the parties are helped to deduce from the agreed-upon propositions what changes in structures, institutions, and policies are required to implement them. At this stage interests surface, especially the interests of those who fear the consequences of change. There is less analysis and far more assertion and defense of positions.

There will be a tendency for the status quo party to be law-and-order oriented and it is necessary to break away from the traditional notions of power, majority control, power balances, human rights conferred on minorities, and other traditional power notions that have led to failure of mediation and negotiation. The role of the panel is twofold: first to make sure the real costs of change and refusal to change are assessed (for example, the likelihood of continued conflict, a deteriorating economy, adverse foreign relations, and so on), and second, to be creative regarding possible options.

Options must be deduced from agreed-upon statements of values. Whatever conclusions emerge as a result of logical deductions from values, they should be translated into policies, institutions, and structures, even ones that seem novel.

> **Rule Forty-nine.** The panel should help the participants to deduce from the agreed-upon propositions those changes in structures, institutions, and policies that are required to carry agreed-upon propositions into effect and should seek discussion on them.

In many cases it will be found that participants are not ready to look ahead to future options. They will discuss the longer-term goals in principle, but they are living in a complex conflict situation that has a momentum of its own, due to vested interests in the conflict itself. It will be necessary to give consideration to transition steps. However, care must be taken to relate transition to ultimate goals so that the former will not destroy the latter.

There is a warning note to be sounded in this regard. In a complex conflict situation there is always a tendency to seek tension-reduction measures as a means to improve confidence and move toward an agreement. Tension-reduction measures, however, can have the opposite effect. They can make the conflict bearable, create role and other interests in the continued conflict, and institutionalize it. While every proposal must be considered on its own merits, this danger needs to be kept in mind.

Rule Fifty. Attempts should be made to arrive at some transition steps that pave the way for longer-term solutions.

At this point the panel has to show imagination. Though there are universal patterns of conflict behavior, each conflict situation has its own unique environmental, cultural, political, and external dimensions. If the conflict involves communities, resolution may be achieved only by a break from traditional institutional forms of government and a consideration of forms of decentralization or zonal systems that border on separation. Similarly in industrial conflicts, some radical changes in structure might seem appropriate, for example, some interactive decision making between management and workforce.

Traditional approaches are usually not helpful. In fact they themselves have given rise to the problem. Options must evolve from the specific needs and interests of the parties and not from some catalogue of available structures. The participants, however, are usually too caught up in their own problems to consider alternative solutions. Usually they do not have the knowledge background to design innovative approaches. The success of the facilitation process will, in large part, depend on the abilities of panel members to come up with possible models for participants to consider. It may be appropriate to illustrate models by symbolic drawings or to make some further elaboration on needs theory and its applications. (A drawing board should be available.)

Rule Fifty-one. The panel must assume a responsibility for putting forward a range of possible options for discussion without putting forward any firm proposals.

Policies

A stage emerges at which it is relevant to discuss policies, especially the policies to be followed during transition from conflict to peace. Typically industry will have been disrupted in a prolonged industrial conflict. In a communal conflict economies will have been destroyed, armed forces will be in control at ground level, and communication will have been disrupted, both physically and behaviorally. The panel will not be informed on local details and it cannot be of much help except to maintain the controlled dialogue.

It may be necessary for the sponsor to make arrangements for many ad hoc seminars on particular issues between those concerned. The sponsor must be guided by the parties, but should not regard the work as complete until discussions on transition policies that look to the future can take place readily between the parties.

> **Rule Fifty-two.** Toward the end of the discussions on values, goals, and structures, the panel should make sure to include a preliminary discussion on transitional policies. It should also find out what special seminars may be required in the future.

Reentry and Follow-up

If circumstances allow, the first seminar series should result in agreement to meet again, and in establishing a means for the parties and the panel to stay in communication. Participants should be asked to agree to relay all communications to all participants, not just to certain selected individuals. Such communications will relate mostly to organizational matters and not to issues of substance.

The reentering parties should be encouraged to establish a base so that they can widen their contacts, and thus both promote the process and prepare the relevant audience to consider the outcomes.

Rule Fifty-three. The panel should ensure adequate time on the last day of a seminar series for discussion of next steps and means of continued communication pending a further meeting.

Both during and between seminar series there is frequently a need for discussion within parties. If participants represent different factions within a party, differences among them will emerge that need to be sorted out before there can be further progress. Sponsors and panel members, aware of time constraints, tend to keep the participants at work in seminars even in evenings. This practice can prove to be dysfunctional. It may also be dysfunctional to convene a seminar series too early. As differences within parties may not come to the notice of the sponsors, a good general rule is to allow free time during a seminar series and to allow the participants to set dates for future meetings.

Rule Fifty-four. The panel must be alert to differences arising within parties and provide time for discussion within and between seminar series. If there are conflicting factions within the parties, it may be necessary to provide for the facilitation of their conflicts before proceeding with another seminar series.

There is a danger that participants will become an in-group and be alientated from others at home who may know less about the process, but who wish to be part of it. As the agenda shifts from one seminar series to another, participants should be changed, with some overlap to ensure continuity and make unnecessary the preliminary steps of initiation into the process.

Rule Fifty-five. Each meeting should build on the last so there is a natural progression from analysis of the conflict, to a deduction of the required political structures, to negotiation of the interests involved in making the required changes, and to the discussion on policies. Participants should be selected accordingly.

A related danger is that the meetings may become institutionalized and have no end point. Although situations vary, generally two or three seminar series should be sufficient to arrive at options for authorities to consider. Any further meetings should be confined to specific aspects of the general problem. Sometimes such ad hoc meetings are best located at the scene of the conflict.

Rule Fifty-six. The panel should always have in mind the earliest possible termination of the seminar series, moving as quickly as possible from definition and options to consideration of consequences and implementation.

Select Bibliography

Alger, C. "Creating Participatory Global Cultures." *Alternatives* 4,4 (Spring 1981).

Banks, M., ed. *Conflict in World Society: A New Perspective on International Relations*. Brighton, Sussex: Wheatsheaf Books Ltd., 1984.

Burgmann, V. *Power and Protest: Movements of Change in Australian Society*. New York: Allen and Unwin, 1993.

Burton, J. *Deviance, Terrorism and War: The Processes of Solving Unsolved Social and Political Problems*. New York: St. Martin's Press, 1979.

———. *Global Conflict*. Brighton, Sussex: Wheatsheaf Books Ltd., 1984.

———. *Conflict: Resolution and Provention*. New York: St. Martin's Press; London: Macmillan, 1990.

Burton, J., and F. Dukes. *Conflict: Practices in Management, Settlements and Resolution*. New York: St. Martin's Press London: Macmillan, 1990.

Chomsky, N. *Deterring Democracy*. New York: Hill and Wang, 1992.

Davies, J. *The Human Nature of Politics*. New York: John Wiley, 1963.

Dukes, F. *Resolving Public Conflict: Transforming Community and Governance*. Manchester: Manchester University Press, 1996.

Green, P. *The Pursuit of Inequality*. New York: Pantheon, 1975.

Jabri, V. *Discourses on Violence: Conflict Analysis Reconsidered*. Manchester: Manchester University Press, 1996.

Kelman, H. "The Problem-Solving Workshop in Conflict Resolution." R. Merritt, ed. *Communication in International Politics*. Chicago: University of Chicago Press, 1972.

Kennedy, P. *Preparing for the Twenty First Century*. New York: Harper and Collins, 1993.

Kwitny, J. *Endless Enemies: The Making of an Unfriendly World*. New York: Congdon and Weed, Inc., 1984.

Lloyd-Bostock, S. "Explaining Compliance with Imposed Law." S. Burman and B. Bond, eds. *The Imposition of Law*. New York: Academic Press, 1979.

Mansbridge, J. *Beyond Adversary Democracy*. New York: Basic Books, 1980.

Maslow, A. *Towards a Psychology of Being*. Princeton: Princeton Press, 1974.

Mitchell, C. *Peacemaking and the Consultant's Role*. Farnborough: Gower; New York: Nichols, 1981.

Mumford, L. "Utopia: The City and the Machine." E. Manuel, ed. *Utopias and Utopian Thought*. New York: Souvenir Press, 1965.

Paige, G. *The Scientific Study of Political Leadership*. New York: Free Press, 1977.

Partridge, P. H. *Consent and Consensus*. London: Pall Mall Press Ltd., 1971.

Rubenstein, R. *Alchemists of Revolution: Terrorism in the Modern World*. New York: Basic Books, 1987.

Sandole, D., and H. Merwe: eds. *Conflict Resolution: Theory and Practice: Integration and Practice*. Manchester: Manchester University Press, 1993.

Sites, P. *Control: The Basis of Social Order*. New York: Dunellen Publishers, 1973.

Tillett, G. *Resolving Conflict: A Practical Approach*. Sydney: Sydney University Press, 1991.

Vasquez, J. *Beyond Confrontation*. Ann Arbor: The University of Michigan Press, 1995.

Index

Pages on which there are definitions of terms are in bold

About the Author

John W. Burton, born in Australia in 1915, received his Ph.D. and D.Sc. from the University of London. His first career was in the Australian Public Service in which he became Secretary of the Department of External Affairs in 1947. He attended the United Nations Charter Conference at San Franscisco in 1945, the Paris Peace Conference in 1946, and many Asian conferences. In 1964 he took a teaching post at University College, London, where he was Director of the Centre for the Analysis of Conflict. In 1979 he moved to the University of Kent, and from 1983 taught at the University of Maryland and George Mason University, Virginia, where he helped to establish Centers for Conflict Analysis and Resolution.

His books include *The Alternative: A Dynamic Approach to Australian Relations with Asia* (Morgan, 1954); *Peace Theory: Pre-conditions of Disarmament* (Knopf, 1962); *International Relations: A General Theory* (Cambridge, 1965); *Systems, States, Diplomacy and Rules* (Cambridge, 1968); *Conflict and Communication: The Use of Controlled Communiction in International Relations* (Macmillan, 1969); *World Society* (Cambridge, 1972); *Deviance, Terrorism and War: A Study in Process in Solving Unsolved Social and Political Problems* (St. Martin's, 1979); *Dear Survivors* (Frances Pinter, 1982); *Global Conflict* (Wheatsheaf, 1983); *Conflict Resolution: Theory and Practice*, with Ed Azar (Wheatsheaf, 1986); *Resolving Deep-rooted Conflict* (University Press of America, 1987), the Conflict Series of four books, two with Frank Dukes (St. Martin's and Macmillan, 1990); and *Violence Explained* (Manchester University Press, 1996).